# CAMBRIDGE ESSAYS
## ON
# ADULT EDUCATION

# CAMBRIDGE ESSAYS

## ON

# ADULT EDUCATION

EDITED BY

## R. ST JOHN PARRY

VICE-MASTER OF TRINITY COLLEGE, CAMBRIDGE

CAMBRIDGE

AT THE UNIVERSITY PRESS

1920

# CAMBRIDGE
## UNIVERSITY PRESS

University Printing House, Cambridge CB2 8BS, United Kingdom

Published in the United States of America by Cambridge University Press, New York

Cambridge University Press is part of the University of Cambridge.

It furthers the University's mission by disseminating knowledge in the pursuit of
education, learning and research at the highest international levels of excellence.

www.cambridge.org
Information on this title: www.cambridge.org/9781107656574

First published 1920
First paperback edition 2014

*A catalogue record for this publication is available from the British Library*

ISBN 978-1-107-65657-4 Paperback

# DEDICATION

## TO THE MASTER OF BALLIOL

DEAR MASTER OF BALLIOL,

In asking you to accept the dedication of this volume of Essays on Adult Education, the contributors have not only had in view the privilege of associating your name with their effort, but have also desired to express their high appreciation of the great services which you have rendered to the cause whose interests they hope to advance, and to record their gratitude for the inspiration which your example and devoted labours have ministered to all who have this cause at heart.

It is a happy omen for the success of the cause and the friendly co-operation of our two Universities that we are allowed to associate the name of so distinguished a member of Oxford University with a volume which appears under the auspices of the Cambridge Press.

I am,

dear Master of Balliol,

most sincerely yours,

THE EDITOR.

CAMBRIDGE,

1 *May* 1920.

# CONTENTS

# CONTENTS

# I

## INTRODUCTION

### By R. St JOHN PARRY

Vice-Master of Trinity College

THE object of this volume of Essays is to bring before the public some of the principal subjects which are dealt with in the Report of the Committee on Adult Education (Cd. 321, 1919). That Report is so far unique in the history of education in Great Britain, as it forms a definite, and to a large extent, exhaustive record of the vast amount of voluntary enthusiasm and effort which has been devoted to the cause of adult education, and asserts principles and makes proposals, which, if whole-heartedly adopted and consistently acted upon, will undoubtedly transform the whole character of the national life. The expression of such a hope may seem to be the dream of an enthusiast. But it is the expression of more than a hope: it marks a widespread and practical effort, actually existing and vigorously supported in every class: and this effort is the culmination of an almost infinite variety of movements, of which the record, given in the Report, covers a period of more than a century. The tide has had its ebbs and flows: but there has been on the whole, a steady advance and an increasing volume. The review of the past and the summary of present conditions alike justify the hope, that the time has come when considered and combined action on the part of the various education authorities may give the opportunity to multiply, in practical ways, effective channels for widespread and deep interest in the better education of people in all ages and classes of the nation.

Our present national conditions emphasise with tremendous force the imperative need for such an advance. Whether we look to our international obligations, or to the mutual relations of that Commonwealth of Nations, which is the new and lasting form of the British Empire, or to our charge of less developed races within the Commonwealth, or to the reorganisation of internal conditions of class relations at home and abroad, it must be obvious to the most casual observer that a high level of knowledge and character must be secured, if the sovereign democracy is not to break down under the burden of its responsibilities. Thoughtful advocates of democracy have from the beginning insisted that democracy can only survive in an educated nation. It may be said that for long the official view has been that such an end can be secured by provision for elementary, secondary, and University education: there has been an implied, if not always explicit, assumption that education ends at the highest with the University, and for the vast majority with the elementary school. But this assumption has never lacked protests. And the protests have become stronger, it is worth observing, with every advance in the provision for the more limited range of education. The foundation must indeed be laid in the schools and colleges for children and adolescents. But the more sane and the more wide-spread this provision grows, the more insistent is the demand for continued, and lifelong education. It is most significant that the passing of the most complete Education Act that this country has yet seen should be practically coincident with this Report, which insists uncompromisingly on the necessity of a comprehensive effort to make it possible that grown-up men and women of all ages and classes may fit themselves, by continued study in subjects as various as human nature itself, to maintain their own personal lives at a high level, and to take everyone his due part in the community of citizens and in the community of mankind.

It may be worth while to call attention to some of the principal assumptions which are made in this Report, and some of the main lines laid down for dealing with its subject.

Perhaps the fundamental assumption is that in all adults there is a capacity for continued education of a high order, granted the right method of approach. This assumption is based upon a double experience. On the one hand, the records of more than a century show a steadily recurring effort of individuals and groups, particularly among the working classes, to secure for themselves the means of such education: and these efforts have had a considerable measure of success, although from various causes particular institutions, in which they have taken form, have from time to time failed in, or departed from, their original object. But a careful consideration of the Historical Survey[1] given in

---

[1] *Report*, Ch. ii. and Appendix I.

# R. St JOHN PARRY

the Report will show that the failures have been due, not to mistakes in the assumption on which the movements were based, but to defective method and lack of adequate experience. The history of the Mechanics' Institutes and of the Working Men's Colleges[1], both in their success and in their failure, illustrates this assertion by way both of warning and of encouragement.

On the other hand, the years of the Great War have given an opportunity for a fresh and most important experiment. Whatever were the faults that attended the experiments made both at the front, and in camps and hospitals at home, it cannot be doubted that there was a very large and genuine response to the educational appeal. The response was not limited to any age or any class of men on service. Some of the most interesting results were obtained in training camps for young conscripts[2]. But even amidst the disturbing conditions of active service during the winter months and the period of demobilisation after the armistice, important evidence was obtained both as to this desire and as to the capacity for continued education.

It may be said, generally, that, while it is admitted that in proportion to the mass of the population the quantitative results have never been more than fractional, there is more than sufficient evidence to support our assumption already on record in all classes throughout the country. Well considered methods have always elicited a most encouraging response. Spon-

[1] See Essay III.

[2] *Report*, pp. 26 f., Appendix I. Part ii and the Second Interim Report Cd. 9225, 1918).

taneous efforts have been frequent over a long period of years.

A second principle, which is maintained in the Report, is the essential importance of trusting and encouraging voluntary effort. It is characteristic of the growth of education in these islands that it has till the last few years depended almost exclusively on voluntary effort, inspired by religious or humanitarian motives. The whole structure of our secondary schools and Universities has sprung from the public spirit and enthusiasm of individuals or groups.

Not till the vast growth of the population and the increasing complexity of later social order outstripped the capacity of voluntary interest, was the assistance of the State invoked: and although it is fully recognised that such assistance is necessary and right, and that the more generous provision which is now being made for it, in all departments of education, is wise and proper, it is maintained that full provision must be made for the continuance and encouragement of the spontaneous service of voluntary enthusiasm, unless we are to cut adrift from our best traditions. Above all in adult education is this essential. For the adult, continuous study depends upon conviction and spontaneity. The grown man or woman cannot be driven to school[1]. The sense of personal need and the sense of public duty must be present; and, if not present, must be aroused. The life conditions of classes, groups and even individuals must form the basis of education[2]; and to take adequate

---

[1] *Report*, pp. 2, 3, §§ (vi) (vii).
[2] See Essay VI.

account of such conditions requires intimate local knowledge and intelligent sympathy. Such a demand cannot be satisfied by a merely official organisation. Voluntary assistance will be required in increasing amount, and in even more intelligent devotion. Further, the temper in which such assistance can alone be satisfactorily cultivated and rendered must colour the necessary official action. It must be fully and generously recognised by the official element as equal partner in the great business. The difficulties of such co-operation are great. But unless they are solved, we shall see the failure of another great educational ideal, and a failure perhaps more disastrous than any we have yet experienced. But there is no reason to be apprehensive on this score. There is every sign in the central authority of the State of a generous recognition both of the necessity and of the essential conditions of adult education: and such signs are not wanting among the local authorities [1]. But the creation and maintenance of the right temper and methods in this co-operation will need constant vigilance and make great demands on the public spirit and devotion of men and women throughout the country.

It may be worth while to dwell briefly on some special characteristics and problems which come into view on a survey of the past and forecast of the future of adult education. One of the most striking features which occurs in almost every experiment recorded is the intense sense of fellowship created by common study spontaneously undertaken. The experience of our

[1] See Essay VIII.

colleges and schools ought to have prepared us to expect this: but in them the *esprit de corps* is inwoven of so many diverse strands, that it is often hard to detect in the completed fabric the strain of common intellectual enthusiasm. In the old Sunday Schools, Adult Schools, Mechanics' Institutes, and in the modern Extension Lectures and Tutorial Classes, it is the thirst for knowledge which is the main bond of union, and it is in the common attempt to satisfy an intellectual need that the sense of fellowship is developed. "We began as students and ended as friends" expresses an almost invariable experience in this kind of class.

Nor is this merely an instance of the natural gregariousness of man. It is the result of enthusiasm shared, and of gains secured by common effort and mutual exchange. Mr Cobham's essay on a Student's Experience brings out this factor with great force. Another essay records the opinion that "a Tutorial Class is not deemed successful unless it produces offspring[1]": the acquisition of their object makes missionaries of the students. This moral or, I would rather say, spiritual quality, which so constantly attends these efforts, is obviously beyond price in our social and national life. It constitutes in itself a stirring appeal to all who have it in their power to give what in the giving produces so fine a flower of character. It holds the promise of the creation of the atmosphere in which there is most hope of a wise solution of our social and national problems.

An essential condition of success in any experiment in adult education is that it should start from, and take

[1] See p. 59 and p. 185.

full account of, the special conditions of life and immediate intellectual requirements of the particular students. This involves beginning with a specialised form of study, which in our regular school and college courses we have been accustomed to put last. But where the effort demanded must be voluntary and spontaneous it is the natural and the only course to take. It is natural that a class of mothers should begin with "The History of the Home[1]": that a class of young conscripts from the woollen trade of Yorkshire should be found interested in the study of wool, its history and its treatment[2]: that economics and the history of industry should be the favourite subjects of Tutorial Classes for working men[3]. The wider implications of this principle are put with great force in Mr Greenwood's essay. This is natural: and experience shows that it is not in any way to be deprecated. "A little knowledge is a dangerous thing": but it is not nearly so dangerous as total ignorance. If the right atmosphere is created in a class, by the sincerity of the students, and mutual trust and sympathy between the students themselves and the student and the tutor, the mental training which is given by the thorough study of a subject, under whatever limitations and even prejudices it is begun, is itself a good thing and may be trusted itself to correct the prejudices and widen the limits within which it began. This is a process within the experience of all who have taken part in such work. The record of

[1] See Essay VII.
[2] *Report*, pp. 2 f.
[3] See Essay IX.

the gradual enlargement of the range of subjects chosen by Tutorial Classes[1] is important evidence.

These considerations raise the burning question of bias: in particular, the question of allowing public assistance to efforts of education inspired by definite sectarian, social or political views and objects. The line which the Committee take on this subject[2] will probably be regarded as the most disputable of all their contentions. They maintain that a scheme, or class, or college, should not be debarred from public assistance merely on the ground that they are primarily devised by, or under the control of, particular interests. This proposition goes counter to traditional educational policy and involves the abandonment of much educational practice. And yet it is based on simple principles. It starts from the assertion that the public authority has to consider, not the institution which does the work, but the quality of the work done: it has to be satisfied as to the competence of the tutor, and the seriousness of the student: if it attempts at the same time to dictate or to proscribe the opinions of tutor or student or of the body under which they work, it is establishing at once a state censorship, in which, when we discover it in another nation, we easily detect a potent source of corruption in the national life. In fact, the fundamental question is raised whether public assistance is consistent with the essential liberty of teaching and liberty of study. The almost exclusively voluntary character of English education in the past, to which attention has already been called, is both a cause and an outcome of suspicion

[1] See Essay IX.  [2] *Report*, §§ 215, 216.

of state interference deep-rooted in the English character. Such a suspicion is amply justified when the
Government itself is in the hands of a class: and the
dangers, which it signals, will always arise when that
is the case, whatever class may be uppermost. Contem-
porary history provides varied instances of this fact.
But to be forewarned is to be forearmed. This is one of
many instances which show that the enemy of freedom
is government by a class in the interests of a class. The
remedy is to oust that enemy from its position, not to
attempt to hedge round particular interests against its
threats, while allowing the central stronghold to be
occupied. Further, the liberty of education must not be
defended by restricting its area. Education itself is
a powerful ally of freedom. It is this quality which
justifies us in claiming a large allowance of public
assistance, in the confidence that an educated people is
the surest guarantee of its own liberties. It is this same
confidence in education which leads us to maintain that
it is itself the antidote to limited views and prejudices in
its promoters. This truth is illustrated by the common
reaction of students against bias in their teachers, and
the as frequent widening of opinion and interests in
both teacher and learners in the progress of their
studies. The essential condition, and the only essential
condition, of public assistance is that the authority
should be satisfied as to the quality of the work done in
relation to the student's opportunities, as to the competence of the tutor and the serious interest of the
students. If we can get this principle established, as the
basis of all state regulation of education, we shall both

secure the recognition and encouragement of all kinds of interests which are concerned, from whatever motives, to promote education and at the same time, trusting to the steady spread of education throughout the nation, meet the dangers of undue state interference with confident equanimity.

Not the least important part of the Report which we are considering, is that which deals with the organisation of adult education. The subject is treated in this volume by Mr Mansbridge, whose experience in the matter is unrivalled. The Report is constructive and covers the whole range: it discusses the place to be taken by the State, the Local Authorities, the Universities, and all kinds of voluntary associations which have education as their one aim, or include it among other objects. It may be allowable here to call attention to the demands made upon the Universities.

The part already taken by the Universities is fully described in the essays by Miss Thompson and Mr Constable which deal with the University Extension system and the Tutorial Classes. On two grounds it is important to secure the continued and enlarged interest of the Universities in adult education beyond their own walls. On the one hand it is essential that any scheme of general education should be in touch with the Universities, if we are to maintain a high standard and a liberal outlook: and on the other hand, the Universities must keep in close touch with the higher educational interests of the nation, if they are to continue to render to the nation one of the most important of their traditional services, in training its ruling classes. The urgency of this demand is only increased by the extension of the responsibilities of government over a wider area[1]. A further and scarcely less, if less, important consideration is that the fruitfulness of the specific and internal business of the Universities, both in education and in the extension of the boundaries of knowledge, is itself not unaffected by the degree in which they are aware of, and at home with, the intellectual, social and industrial movements in the world at large.

The most important contributions which the Universities have to make to the general interests of adult education are the provision of highly-qualified and sympathetic teachers, the securing of sound method and thoroughness in study, and the establishment by these means of a standard of education in the higher ranges, which will affect the temper and the quality of all the work, even of those parts with which the Universities themselves are not directly concerned.

In submitting these and the like considerations, the Report of the Committee[2] urges upon the notice of Universities the responsibility of giving this part of their work an established place in their system, adequately equipped with administrative facilities, and financed proportionately to its importance. Their first suggestion is that the whole business of extramural education should be put in charge of a University body, such as is in the several Universities appointed to take charge of and promote a main department of University work. In the second place, it is strongly urged that the nature of this work makes it essential

---

[1] See Essay V.          [2] See §§ 165 ff.

that on such a body the interests of the student and other bodies closely connected with the work should be directly represented, even though the representatives are not themselves members of the University. This arrangement has no lack of precedents and is devised to secure an intimate knowledge of the special needs concerned. In regard to finance, while the Committee hold that the main burden of finance must be borne by the public authorities and voluntary associations, they still urge that some financial responsibility should be undertaken by the University as a guarantee of its interest in the work, and an additional security for the independence of its influence on the methods of its execution.

It is obvious that in all this, a great demand is made upon the Universities: but it is encouraging to reflect that the demand is itself largely due to the past and present action of the Universities themselves. The current activities of adult education in its higher forms are to a large extent the result of stimulus issuing from the Universities and dependent upon their aid. It is not altogether a new burden imposed upon them from without, but the natural result of missionary work in education originating from within. The highest reward of service is a demand for more service.

To meet this demand the main difficulties will not lie in the matter of administration, which is already or can be, without much change, provided. They lie in the direction of the supply of teachers and finance. On both these lines there is one essential condition, and that is the vivid recognition that the supply of a sound and

adequate system of adult education is of the highest
national, and more than national, importance. To this
point I have already addressed myself: and it may be
said to be the undercurrent of all the essays of this
volume. Granted this recognition, we may reasonably
anticipate that the call of public service will lead many
of our keenest students to see in this direction the
opportunity of response: and that the provision of
opportunities of training and of an adequate livelihood
for those who adopt this line of work will meet the
difficulty of the supply of teachers.

The provision of an adequate livelihood is a matter of
finance. Both the older and the newer Universities at
present find themselves in a situation in which the
maintenance and the indispensable developments of
their primary duties of intra-mural education and of the
promotion of knowledge and research demand a very
large increase of the funds at their disposal, large, that
is, in proportion to their present resources however
carefully husbanded. It may be argued that, this being
the case, the present is no time for attempting to meet
further responsibilities. But that is not an argument
which can be wisely entertained by responsible authorities. The case for larger assistance from public sources
and from private benefactions depends upon the urgency
of the service, which the Universities can claim to
render. And at the present time, as this volume
endeavours to show in conjunction with the Report of
the Adult Education Committee, no service is more
urgent, or more hopeful, in the interests of knowledge
no less than in the interests of the nation, than that of

widespread adult education. In this service it is a matter of extreme urgency that the Universities should be enabled to take their proper and full part.

At the present time claims are being made on behalf of all the Universities for increased assistance from public funds; and these claims are being considered by the State, and, in the case of Oxford and Cambridge, by the Royal Commission lately appointed. In justifying the claims, the needs of University responsibilities for extra-mural adult education should be clearly stated and strongly pressed. It would also be in accordance with our general argument for the co-operation of official and voluntary agency that this sphere of opportunity should be brought before the notice of possible benefactors.

In concluding these introductory remarks, I may be allowed to express my thanks to all my colleagues in the production of this volume, for the ready kindness and promptitude with which they have given their assistance, in the midst of other pressing labours and often under considerable difficulties. The essays stand as they were first written, with in most cases no revision, and in no case any but very slight revision, on the part of the Editor. The unity of principle and spirit which will be found to pervade the essays depends, not on editorial supervision, but upon our common interest in a great cause, and coincidence of individual experience in its several departments. Our aim will be fulfilled if the publication of this volume leads to a wider and deeper study of the Report of the Committee on Adult Education.

# II

# THE PURPOSE AND MEANING OF
# ADULT EDUCATION

## By D. H. S. CRANAGE

Secretary of the Cambridge University Local Lectures

FEW words have covered more shades of meaning than
"education." As used by some it would indicate little
more than the bald facts taught to small children, but by
some it seems to embrace almost all the activities of life.
By derivation, however, as well as by worthy use, it
means much more than the learning of facts; it is in
addition the bringing out of latent powers and the
process of training—spiritual, moral, intellectual, and
physical. But in general custom it is connected almost
entirely with children and adolescents. Even the new
*Concise Oxford Dictionary of Current English* gives, as the
first meaning of the word, "bringing up (of the young)."
It is a correct definition, demanded by " current
English," if not by derivation and idealism. By such
a definition " adult education " is a contradiction in
terms, and we must therefore get away from it, if we are
to arrive at a true ideal of the process which must
continue through life if human powers are to be fully
developed.

Argument is surely unnecessary to prove that education should not cease when adult age is attained. By
that time it is true that most people have been prepared

to earn some sort of living, but the most selfish of motives would dictate a higher attainment than this, and it is stupid to be satisfied with it. It is, however, just as stupid to suppose that when "young ladies" have been to a "finishing school" their education is complete. Nearly everyone is the better for some technical training, after school age is past, if material success alone is aimed at; but I am concerned with quite other considerations in this essay. Let us think of adult education as including the whole being, whether it increases the money-earning powers or not. The first Lord Goschen spoke of it as the "means of life" rather than the "means of livelihood." From this point of view it is obvious that education is only begun in childhood. We may think ourselves fortunate if, when we come of age, our minds have been trained to learn quickly and wisely, even if our stock of knowledge is still small. By that time in an ideal case, almost to be compared with Macaulay's schoolboy, two things will have happened. The weapons of the mind will have been sharpened to a fine edge, and a sound foundation of knowledge will have been laid in language, history, literature, art, science, to say nothing of the most important requisite, the training of character. But, even in such an ideal case, education must be continued in the adult or the powers gained in the child will be atrophied through disuse. There is a striking passage in the autobiographical chapter of Charles Darwin's *Life*[1]:

Up to the age of thirty, or beyond it, poetry of many kinds, such as the works of Milton, Gray, Byron, Wordsworth,

[1] *Life of Charles Darwin* (London, 1902), pp. 50-51.

Coleridge and Shelley, gave me great pleasure, and even as a schoolboy I took intense delight in Shakespeare, especially in the historical plays....But now, for many years, I cannot endure to read a line of poetry: I have tried lately to read Shakespeare, and found it so intolerably dull that it nauseated me. I have also almost lost my taste for pictures or music....My mind seems to have become a kind of machine for grinding general laws out of large collections of facts, but why this should have caused the atrophy of that part of the brain alone, on which the higher tastes depend, I cannot conceive...if I had to live my life again, I would have made a rule to read some poetry, and listen to some music at least once every week; for perhaps the parts of my brain now atrophied would thus have been kept active through use. The loss of these tastes is a loss of happiness, and may possibly be injurious to the intellect, and more probably to the moral character, by enfeebling the emotional part of our nature.

What can be a stronger argument than this for adult education? It is a sad reflection that, for want of it, many a man at 40 is less effective, less sympathetic, less interesting, than he was at 20. If Darwin had to admit that he had gone back in important respects, lesser men may well take warning.

For the moment I have been dealing with the ideal case, where a person reaches adult age as perfectly equipped as possible. Even there continued education is a necessity. But the large majority have no pretensions to be so perfectly equipped. Apart from mere knowledge most of us need more "mental gymnastics" than we got in childhood. This can be given by the continued and systematic study of any subject, under wise direction. Some subjects are doubtless better than others for this purpose, but any subject can be educational, quite apart from the knowledge it conveys. It would not be fair to say that we can get no sound learning, till we have been through such a serious discipline, but without it we shall always be handicapped in acquiring knowledge and in conveying it to others. Training, however, must not end, as Pope has it, in

> Tricks to show the stretch of human brain,
> Mere curious pleasure, or ingenious pain.

The trained mind must quickly go on to acquire varied knowledge, for its own health and for the good of others. Who would not admit the intense need in his own case? It is not too much to say that we are all losing daily in power, in usefulness, in happiness, by our ignorance of vast fields of knowledge. What extraordinary gaps there are in the equipment of "educated" persons! I remember speaking to one who seriously thought that an engine-driver had to guide his engine across points in the same way that a chauffeur drives his car across a road. It is not many years ago since a well known publicist spoke in the House of Commons of "the island of Poland." Most of us have probably gone through the experience of being shocked again and again by the revelation of our own ignorance in important matters.

There are, however, many who freely admit their ignorance, and yet see no necessity for removing it. "Education" has been a painful process with them, and "adult education" would prolong the misery through life. The teaching of such an one must have been terribly mismanaged in childhood, but the case is still far too common. In the new continuation schools, the compulsory age will be prolonged to 16 and then to 18, by which time it may be hoped, under improved methods of teaching, that nearly all will see the beauty of knowledge. However, sooner or later, all compulsion must be withdrawn, and adult education must be essentially voluntary. It must make its appeal therefore to the will, I had almost said to the conscience, of the individual, with little or no help from authority.

What then is the purpose of adult education? What is the justification for spending time, money, and energy, upon it? As applied to the whole community it is almost a new idea, and for long it will have to struggle against the lazy shallowness, which takes refuge in such catchwords as "a little knowledge is a dangerous thing" or even "when ignorance is bliss, 'tis folly to be wise." There are the strongest moral reasons why, on personal and social grounds, adults should continue their education, but human nature is so constituted that such reasons must be reinforced by an appeal to the imagination and the interest. Take a simple case. Everyone nowadays travels. "A day in the country" or "a day at the seaside" is generally brought within the reach of those who cannot do more. At such a time, interest can easily be aroused by a wise friend. The char-à-banc passes a lofty exposure of rock in Derbyshire: an explanation of the why and the wherefore follows and the casual observer may become the life student. Fountains Abbey is visited in a picnic and holiday mood: a mere picturesque ruin becomes eloquent of the Middle Ages and English history is ever after clothed with romance. The north coast of

Cornwall is the goal of an excursion: as the Atlantic waves roll in, Byron's address to the Ocean is recalled, and for the first time poetry lives. In these and a hundred other ways intellectual interest may be aroused. The occasion may be ordinary and commonplace, but the influence may be lasting if exercised with sympathy and simplicity. At the beginning of the day nothing was further from the thoughts than a course of adult education; at the end such a course may have begun unconsciously. Simple instances of this kind may bring home the importance of the matter from the point of view of personal happiness. What a poor stunted thing a life must be which has no sense of the wonders of nature, no interest in history, no feeling for art, no response to literature! At best, only the beginnings of these things are imparted in childhood. Much of the happiness of life depends on their progressive development. Their absence may not be noticed in the middle of a busy career, but, when illness and old age come on, the poverty of an uneducated mind becomes painfully evident. How full the declining days may be, and how empty they often are! The Homeric studies of Mr Gladstone may have lengthened his life; they certainly added much to its enjoyment.

As a mere hobby then, some special study may contribute much to health and happiness, but I should be sorry to rest the case for adult education entirely, or even mainly, upon such an argument. If its basis is purely selfish, it cannot make much progress in an age when service for others is so widely recognized. Fortunately it is not so. Over and over again I have noticed that the leaders of religious and social movements who really influence their fellows are those who have consistently supported higher education and obtained the benefit of it themselves. Without it a man may be earnest and good, but the earnestness is apt to degenerate into fanaticism and the goodness into pride and priggery. Sympathy is not possible apart from knowledge, and without sympathy little can be done to help others. I have met religious and philanthropic workers who would dearly like to attend to the things of the mind, but who feel it a duty, with sin and misery around them, to devote their whole time to their special work. It is a mistaken renunciation and means the throwing away of a powerful weapon for effecting the main purpose. No one needs the help of adult education more than the man whose life is spent in trying to raise others. The responsibility of parents is specially great in these days of new knowledge, which is apt to cause a breach between the older and younger generations. Nothing can quite make up to a child for the lack of cultured intercourse with a well-educated father and mother.

Consider first the religious teacher. What are the qualities which go to make success? No doubt mainly goodness, earnestness, sincerity; but the faithful teacher will add to his virtue knowledge. Many a man drifts into unbelief by refusing to examine the foundations of his faith. Who can help him better than one who has diligently been through the process and come out triumphant? A teacher, however virtuous, who is content to repeat old formulas without full knowledge of their meaning, will not help his own faith, much less that of others. Further, a teacher who is content with a narrow basis of knowledge, however exact in itself, will not have much influence. Men and women vary in their powers and their temperaments. The teacher who would reach their inmost souls must have many lines of approach. Any good preacher would say that he has found every sort of knowledge useful, and that the more he adds to it the more effective he becomes. Breadth is necessary as well as depth. The greatest Teacher who ever lived took His illustrations from nature, from history, from literature. Spiritual truth was always the centre, but the setting was often earthly and depended for its effect on its varied appeal.

The teacher of any subject must go on with his own studies or he will soon lose the power of inspiring others. His pupils, whether children or adults, will quickly notice if he is repeating, like a gramophone, statements which he has learnt long before, or if he is giving out from a full heart truths which he is continually making his own. A living teacher must have vast reserves of knowledge which are seldom displayed, and such reserves are effective only if he is constantly adding to and reviving them. None are more enthusiastic in the cause of adult education than teachers, not merely because of its importance to the general public, but because they feel the vital need of it for themselves.

Think too of the political and social worker. Many a man is elected to Parliament, to a Town or County Council, or to a Board of Guardians, while he still has the haziest idea of its responsibilities. It would, I suppose, be a counsel of perfection to suggest, that everyone elected to such offices should pass some test of knowledge before being allowed to act. None the less painstaking study becomes the solemn duty of every member. Fortunately most people are willing to defer to their colleagues who have knowledge. There is no more striking example of the saying that knowledge is power than the deference paid to the expert on such a body. But this does not lessen the duty of all to fulfil the trust committed to them by equipping themselves with at least sufficient knowledge to enable them to understand the reasons of the expert. Such knowledge is gained to a small extent in childhood. Without adult education, therefore, our national and municipal affairs will be managed ignorantly, our poor will not be treated with wisdom and sympathy.

Not less urgent is the case of the trades union leader, and no class is recognizing more forcibly the need of higher education. As with the religious teacher, it is character which tells most, but knowledge is almost as important, knowledge so varied that one can imagine the serious man to be abashed by its complexity. A modern trade has so many ramifications that, to understand it, a good knowledge is required of history, of geography, of economics, of science. In addition, and more difficult still, there must be a close understanding of "Labour." What does this mean but human nature? for in all classes and in all ages, the nature of man is much the same. We are driven back again to the need of sympathy based on knowledge. A trades union leader will be saved from many mistakes if he studies psychology, which may be the most important science of the twentieth century, but apart from that he will gain enormously if his knowledge is broad as well as deep. There will be countless chances for its use in his dealings with both masters and men, not merely to impress with a vulgar sense of power, but to overcome real difficulties which ignorance cannot remove. Once more, this knowledge is not reached in childhood. Happy is the man who soon finds out its importance and sets himself with determination to rise to it. The best labour leaders have been very willing to submit themselves to mental discipline, in childhood perhaps, but certainly in adult life.

The equipment for business, whether conducted for private profit or on co-operative principles, may be thought to be so largely technical that it has no place in this essay, but even technical training if intelligently pursued has a liberalizing effect. In business, too, as well as other activities, a wise decision often depends less on technicalities than on general knowledge of men and things, knowledge which a man will not have who "finished" his education as a youth. Such a thought leads us naturally to the conviction that, whatever one's work or position may be, real efficiency cannot be attained without wide knowledge, not for the teacher only, but for the taught, for the elector as well as the elected, for the led as well as the leader.

This truth is most prominent now, when we consider the problems of political life. We are committed in England to a great democratic experiment: the franchise is being extended to almost all adults of both sexes. If the world is to be safe for democracy, democracy must be educated. How can it be otherwise than dangerous to give great power to the ignorant? It is, however, too late to argue that it would have been safer to educate first and to confer power afterwards. It has never been our English custom to let power wait on education. We have boldly trusted new classes from time to time with responsibility, and it may fairly be claimed that up to now the experiment has been justified. A huge electorate must be accepted as an accomplished fact, and, in the slang phrase, it is "up to us" to see that it is educated. One trembles to think what the result of ignorance may be. Our priceless heritage in religion, in civilization, in accumulated experience, would seem at times to be at the mercy of an uninstructed popular vote. The timid may feel that such things will be destroyed by those who know not what they do. Fortunately the British people have often had the common sense to preserve things they have not fully understood; they have felt it better to make mistakes that way than the other. Undue preservation can be cured later on; undue destruction is irrevocable.

"Le Roy le veult"—the King's parliamentary assent still given in Norman French—is typical of much in England besides legislative procedure. But it is well that institutions should depend on knowledge as well as on racial conservatism. There can be no security for them unless they are both good, and widely known and realized to be good. Our domestic problems have never seemed more overwhelming than at the present time— the relations between capital and labour, Ireland, housing, the drink traffic, transport, public health, to say nothing of education itself. To solve them, character and goodwill are the first requisites, though quite inadequate without knowledge. History is the most obvious help. For example, how can Ireland be understood without it? It may of course be wrongly used. On the one hand a slavish regard for it may help to stereotype a bad system, on the other hand disappointment at its record of failure may lead to experiments merely because they are new. But who can doubt that, if wisely studied, history will create a judicial attitude of mind and save from glaring errors?

Economics is a sister science, for economic theory is a dangerous weapon unless checked by economic history. In no department of knowledge is a superficial treatment more fatal. There are some subjects which a teacher can impart passably by keeping a page ahead of his pupil, but economics, in some of its branches, had better not be taught at all than be in the hands of one who has not mastered its many-sided character. For all such domestic problems adult education is a vital necessity. Even if the foundations have been laid in youth, the mere time required for their study, apart from the maturity needed for their solution, would dictate a prolonged period.

All this is even more true with regard to international problems. The great war has shown very clearly the folly of taking a parochial view of politics. The truth has been borne in upon all of us that the condition of the peoples in central and eastern Europe is a vital concern of Englishmen. Knowledge indeed is needed to help us to bear our responsibility. Take for instance the southern Balkan districts, where one village is Serbian, the next Bulgarian, and others near Albanian. The difficulty will not yield to the talisman of "self-determination," which, good in its essence, becomes a mere catchword in such cases. No solution of some problems can be perfect. Many a pretty theory in state-making is shattered by the sight of a raised map or by some knowledge of differences in religion, race, and language. The wise statesman will take all the evidence into account, and not expect the conditions of the west to be exactly reproduced in the east. It may be urged that the complexity of the problems is so great that they ought to be left to the trained diplomatist. To some extent this must be true, but experts differ in these matters as well as others, and our English way is for the layman to decide. The diplomatist will be far more likely to do right, if he has an instructed public opinion to reckon with at home.

If then we want to make democracy a success we must study these things carefully and not merely read paragraphs about them in our favourite newspapers. If such study is lacking, a powerful bureaucracy is the only security against disaster. There is no substitute for knowledge. If democracy is ignorant, it will in the end have to give way to some other ruling power.

Science is another matter which must not be left entirely to experts. Even great discoveries are not always the unaided work of the expert, but rather the last of thousands of small observations. Not only so, but the expert works better if he is supported by a mass of intelligent opinion. A nation can scarcely believe in science without a good knowledge of it; and, if the nation does not believe, the expert loses one of his strongest supports. This is so with applied science, from which so many things have come which minister to health, power, and commerce. It is even more the case with pure science, the advantage of which cannot be appreciated by a nation lacking in the scientific spirit. It is not long since the British Association set on foot an enquiry into the provision for popular scientific education. Some of its correspondents made the disquieting statement that there was less general interest in the matter than formerly. The celebrated expositions by Tyndall and Huxley were followed by lectures under the Gilchrist Trust and by more systematic work conducted by Universities and by Technical Institutes, but, in the opinion of some, there is not the same healthy excitement about the matter that there was in the last generation. Adult education must remedy this; for it is evident that the more widespread teaching of science in schools is not enough by itself.

A love of good literature is best implanted in youth; for one cannot too soon begin to refuse the evil and to choose the good; but many arrive at adult age without any literary feeling at all, partly through bad teaching, partly because the faculty, like other powers, is often long in developing. Some people, it is true, seem to have no power of appreciating poetry, or indeed good prose, just as some are colour blind; but I believe that nearly everyone can learn from an inspiring teacher. Such teachers are unfortunately rare; but there can be no question that a general diffusion of literary feeling is vital to the health of the republic of letters. We are all the while deploring the huge output of trash, but the reason is that taste is confined to the few, who rage idly at the blindness of the many. Adult education is the remedy, and the subject is peculiarly suited to it. There is no place for the mere pedagogue. Adults will never stand him, and, in literature especially, the teacher should be a humble and reverent fellow-learner with the taught. In the present economic condition of the world the future of the literary man seems none too bright. We may rightly condemn the old patronage of the nobility, with the servile attitude it engendered, but it gave to the world many a literary masterpiece which otherwise would never have seen the light. Let us see to it that our more self-respecting age produces finer results. Voluntary societies, in this as in other branches of adult education, have done much. Are they always so active as they used to be? The general interest in literature is a very fair index of fine literary output.

The drama is a closely allied subject. The instinct for it, like the literary faculty, is a powerful weapon for good or evil. The demand for an endowed theatre seems like a confession of failure. It may be necessary in the present condition of taste; but, if we raise the general level of education, it will surely be possible for a sufficient number of people to find recreation in noble drama, so that a "repertory theatre" will be a commercial as well as an artistic success. Recent experiments in this direction are very encouraging.

Art of course includes literature and the drama, but something must be said about it here in the more usual sense of the word. In no department of life is a high general level of education more important, for popular encouragement is to the artist almost as breath to the nostrils. Great works were wrought by Pheidias and Praxiteles, but they would not have been possible without the enthusiasm of the Greek people. The names of the mediaeval master-builders have often quite disappeared, for the Gothic cathedrals were a reflection of the whole age; they were possible only to a nation which believed in art and was willing to sacrifice itself for it. Such belief is impossible without knowledge, and knowledge of art is not a matter of books only or the Middle Ages would have had little of it. At the present day we have the enormous advantage of time-saving machinery, but this has involved the sad decay of craftsmanship. Education, for children and adults, can set this right. A carpenter's shop is now expected in a well-equipped school, but craft education in some form should go on through life, especially for mental workers, not only for its own sake but as a relief for tired nerves and brains. It is the greatest mistake to identify art with painting and sculpture. They may be its highest form, but they have not the constant importance of craftsmanship. We may have to do without pictures and carvings, but we are obliged to have tables and chairs and beds and clocks. Their workmanship and form often leave much to be desired. Sometimes in a chest no drawer that is shut will open and no drawer that is open will shut. The appearance of modern furniture often makes one shudder. Arts and Crafts exhibitions set before us some things of great beauty, but they appeal only to the few. The large majority buy something very inferior, partly, no doubt, because it is cheaper, but partly because they have not realized the difference between good and bad craftsmanship. Elaboration is not necessary and much money is wasted upon it: some of the simplest objects of daily use can show the best art. We ought to have beautiful and well-made things through the ordinary commercial channels, and not only in sporadic exhibitions. In the last few years there has certainly been an improvement, but who can say that there is not still great need for it? A nation which endures glaring advertisements all along its countryside can scarcely have had a right education in art, either at school or in later life.

Music has a strong social appeal and that alone would make it specially suited to adult education. The appreciation of good music, which the soldiers have recently shown, when properly approached, has been a most encouraging sign. The revival of folk music and dancing is a healthy antidote to much that is stupid or worse.

I have ended with the subject which can best be enjoyed in common, and this leads me to say that the greatest value perhaps of adult education is the fellowship which springs from it. What a difference there is in the home if all the members of a family are engaged in various studies, bringing their experiences into the common stock, and widening the sympathies of all! In greater or less degree the same is true of any community united by common work and still more by common tastes. An association of students, drawn from every class, creed, and party, is one of the best solvents of bitterness and misunderstanding.

Till recently, large sections of our people were cut off from the opportunities I have been describing by lack of leisure, and there are still many whose work leaves them little time or energy for other pursuits. Over-pressure, however, is far less common than it was, so that it becomes a matter of vital concern for the State that the leisure of its citizens shall be wisely spent. This is impossible without varied opportunities for organized adult education. Some, of course, can fill up their time to the best advantage entirely by their own efforts, but most people need friendly direction or their pursuits become desultory. As the movement is wholly voluntary the direction cannot succeed unless it is thoroughly good, not less from the human than from the learned standpoint. However high the academic record of the teacher may be, he will fail if unsympathetic: the students must be associated with him in the direction of their studies. There must be no element of patronage in adult education. The teacher is not placed on a pedestal; he may indeed be inferior in many respects to his students as he will often be in age. Adult education is not only for the promising "young person," but for men and women of any age and position engaged in the ordinary occupations of life. I have known excellent students over 70 years of age. Those who are looked up to by their neighbours can do a special service to the movement by throwing themselves heartily into it on equal terms with others. As fellow-seekers after truth there will be an equality among the students, unsurpassed in any department of life. Which of us can afford to despise the knowledge gained in this way? The specialist must often work alone, but specialized study is not the whole duty of the student. There is much wisdom in the old ideal of knowing "everything about something and something about everything." The latter process at any rate can often be best pursued in association with others. It is never safe to lay down a law for all cases, but I am firmly convinced that most of us would be the better for a systematic attempt to learn in common. I look back on such realized opportunities with gratitude and wish there had been more of them. We are all apt to think we have no time for continued education, but the question to answer is surely not "have I the time?" but "is it worth the time?" We are generally careful to make the time for fresh air, exercise, holidays, as we soon find that our bodily health suffers if we do not. Mental health is not less important, but the lack of it does not come home to us in the same way, however apparent it may be to our friends. People have a wonderful faculty of making time for the things they want to do; if they do not include education, it is because they are not convinced of its value and importance.

The *meaning* of adult education, then, is the continued effort to learn by those past school age whether busily employed or not in earning their livelihood; its *purpose* is to produce and sustain the healthy mind in the healthy body. It can go on daily by thought, by observation, by reading, by making, and it has a special value if pursued in common with others. Life will be infinitely richer for it; sympathy will be quickened, selfishness will shrink, false pride will be subdued. The thing is worth doing; let us do it!

# III

# HISTORICAL SURVEY

## By A. E. DOBBS

Author of *Education and Social Movements 1700—1850*

M͏ʀs P͏ʀᴏᴜᴅɪᴇ once interrupted a lecture at a Mechanics' Institute, causing her husband to jump in his chair; and there is no saying what virtue may lie in a declaration of policy uttered by a bold familiar voice; for out of such interruptions public opinion is formed. A hundred years ago, when steam-power was gathering the population into masses, public opinion was in the making and the destiny of these masses provided a controversial topic. They engaged the attention of philanthropists who desired to restore order and contentment, of employers who were concerned about industrial efficiency, of Robert Owen and the party of social regeneration, of economists who hid their idealism under a bushel of prudence, and of political reformers who were consoled by the prospect of an educated democracy. If all these had been assembled for mutual interruption, I doubt not the public would have gone away with its head full of educational projects—schools for the young and the diffusion among adults of useful knowledge, a fine oracular phrase which promised science to the artisan, enlightenment to the citizen and to one and all "rational amusement." There would have been included the thought of equal opportunities for all classes, which may be read, with comments, in James Mill's treatise on Education (1824). How, he asked, were moral claims to be reconciled with economic necessities? How was society to provide for its livelihood without robbing a "large portion of mankind" of the leisure and energy required for mental improvement? To such questions it would "in time...appear that a most consolatory answer may be given."

The times were full of consolatory answers, plans for the diffusion of elementary and all kinds of knowledge and for improving the spare moments of a busy life. While religious workers in night school and Sunday school offered rudimentary instruction to old as well as young, there developed during the second quarter of the nineteenth century an ambitious scheme of higher popular education inspired by the scientific discoveries of the age and their reactions on industry. The history of the Mechanics' Institutes goes back to the year 1799, when Dr Birkbeck started lecturing to artisans at Glasgow. Both then and in 1824, when he took part in inaugurating the London Institute, he laid stress on the pleasures rather than on the uses of scientific knowledge; but as the movement spread through the manufacturing districts the professional training of artisans became one of its primary aims. Sixty years later, when the teaching of science had revived, some of the original Institutes were incorporated in a municipal system of technical instruction; and the same development awaited societies of more recent growth, which the Yorkshire Union of Institutes had brought into existence. Meanwhile almost at the outset of the movement, as the first enthusiasm declined, a more prominent place had been given to the elements of "general culture" and "mental relaxation" which are mentioned in some of the earlier programmes. At different centres classes in French and other languages and lectures on literature and history, if not part of the original scheme, were introduced in the hope of conciliating public support. Some of the larger Institutes developed concerts, excursions, social meetings and other familiar accessories of adult education. They were pioneers, to some extent, in the education of women; and they opened a career to a new class of professional lecturers, men of high attainments who went on circuit, like the University teachers of later years, discoursing on history, literature, and science, and forming miscellaneous friendships. On the other hand reports on the movement are full of instructive criticism, and about 1850 the position was reviewed in two valuable surveys published by the Society of Arts.

By this time the character of the Institutes had changed with the failure of their original aims. Comparatively few of their members belonged to the working classes, and only a small proportion were genuine students. Courses of study had given place to disconnected lectures; classes in drawing and design were common, but science had fallen into the background; most of the instruction was in elementary subjects, and many of those who attended were juveniles. The defective state of elementary limited the demand for higher education, and in institutions with no assured income it had been difficult to deal fairly with small minorities who might have provided a nucleus of serious students; but it is possible that the failure to educate adults was due in some measure to a confusion of aims. The more efficient Institutes were developing on the lines of a continuation school, and reformers looked forward to an authoritative scheme of studies with regular examinations and suitable awards. The great incentive to study was the prospect of success in life, those who had risen to eminent positions being set up continually as a model for young artisans. Such motives had a natural connexion with vocational training, but they were not sufficient if the movement aimed also at affording culture to mature adults. These are as often won by comradeship as by the hope of preferment; and to pursue a scholastic curriculum is not their natural instinct. Like babies, they desire to feel at home, to have attention paid them, to be allowed to ask questions, and to choose which toys they shall play with. Unfortunately the social side of the Institutes had developed as education declined; the classes were somewhat frigid functions; and the demand for science was limited. Work-people, as the libraries showed, preferred politics and poetry to treatises on the steam-engine. They were often at this time interested in science, but not necessarily in branches connected with their trades, while it required a good lecturer to do the subject justice. And we must remember that the Institutes grew up in years of hunger and unrest. In the quiet 'fifties, when the Government set men like Huxley to lecture in Jermyn Street, artisans attended in hundreds, many staying after the lesson to have their difficulties explained.

Though in 1850 classes were reported to have
declined, there is evidence during the next decade,
especially in the north, of a steady increase in attendance. This is partly to be explained by the formation
of County Unions in the 'forties which, having failed
to organise courses of lectures, opened new fields
of experiment by means of circulating libraries, promoted village centres and drew together societies of
different types. In the large towns there were numerous
examples of working class clubs which had broken off
deliberately from the Mechanics' Institutes, while the
institutes in small towns and villages compared favourably with those in the great centres as regards their hold
on the population and the proportion of their members
who took an active interest in the work. Many of them
had been formed by humble folk desirous of instruction,
and would be more accurately classed with the mutual
improvement societies which multiplied in the industrial
districts during the later 'forties. These smaller groups
had the advantage of a close connexion with some
definite social unit—a compact neighbourhood, a
factory or a circle of friends—of complete freedom, and
of a sociable spirit aroused by the devotion of fellow-
workers to a common task. Depending almost entirely
on mutual aid for the means of instruction they were
often transient formations, though in not a few instances
the members carried on for a period of years, gradually
extending the sphere of their activities and developing
symptoms of idealism. Thus at Leeds four workmen
meeting for elementary instruction formed the nucleus
of a society which organised a discussion circle and
classes in French and Chemistry. At Aberdeen the

members of an essay club turned themselves into a
"College" and proceeded to study Arithmetic, English,
Drawing, Euclid and Latin with the help of a Grammar
School lad. Every Friday evening "our chemist" or
another member lectured, and in the "vacation" they
arranged botanical excursions. In the end they con-
gratulated themselves on having made friends. Such
are the beginnings of adult education. Sometimes, as
in the study circles of recent years, attention was
devoted to some subject of special interest. The naturalist
clubs of Manchester and East London were groups of
serious students who pursued their researches, occasionally under the guidance of a teacher, on holiday rambles
and by visiting museums; at Chorlton, near Manchester,
a few mill hands started a class in French and subscribed
for a French journal; and about 1849 the young men
of Birmingham formed a society to "investigate the
principles of political questions."

It had been a common objection to the Mechanics'
Institutes that they excluded controversy, working men
being desirous, as they expressed it, to be informed of
their rights and duties as citizens. We read continually
of abandoned classes and crowded newsrooms, of indifference to science and a great demand for "political
histories." Political education in a broad sense was
implied in the Benthamite tradition of public enlightenment, and much had been expected of the work of
elementary schools, supplemented in later life by free
debate and the diffusion of useful knowledge. Lovett
who represented the intellectual side of Chartism went
a step further, publishing in 1837 the first democratic
programme of national education, and including in the

curriculum for the higher grades, or "Colleges," political economy and the science of government. But the time had hardly arrived for the organisation of this field of study. The political studies which have played latterly an important part in adult education were to derive their value from the exercise of critical faculties and a patient scrutiny of all available sources of evidence. They presupposed conditions which developed gradually in later years—the type of responsibility which grows with the discharge of civic duties, a more intelligent sympathy between educationalists and popular movements, and the development of research in such subjects as economics and industrial history. The work of Robert Owen and the leaders of early democratic movements does not lose its significance, if it is found to have been in the main of a preliminary nature, if it consisted largely in asserting a right to organise and to express opinions, in forming character, and in connecting education with an ideal of social progress.

### 1850 TO 1900

In the middle years of the century the State was beginning to supervise the growth of elementary schools and at the same time to exercise an influence over the education of adults. The Museum and Library Acts of 1845 and 1850 were followed by the appointment of Commissions to report on the Universities of Oxford and Cambridge, by the offer of grants in aid of elementary evening classes and by the formation in 1853 of a Science and Art Department which became a branch of the central authority. Voluntary enterprise could

show a similar record of small but significant beginnings
—a People's College founded at Sheffield in 1842 which
was afterwards reorganised by the students and
suggested the Working Men's Colleges of the next
decade, the re-birth of co-operation at Rochdale in 1844,
and a movement connected with the Society of Friends
which led to the revival and development of Adult
Sunday Schools. Meanwhile the nation was entering on
a period of prosperity after years of unusual commotion
and distress, the transition being illustrated by two
spectacular events which are also landmarks in educational history. If the Great Exhibition of 1851, by
emphasising the intellectual factor in industrial competition, prepared the way for future schemes of
technical education which offered training for a career,
the Chartist Demonstration of 1848 gave rise cir-
cuitously to a movement for educating adults in subjects
and by methods, which have no immediate connexion
with the task of earning a livelihood and are useful only
in making them better citizens and better men.

During the hungry 'forties many realised for the first
time some of the issues raised by the Industrial Revolution. Society was no longer what Coleridge would have
described as a "moral unit"; classes were divided; and
the physical degradation of large masses of the people
challenged a philosophy of life which accepted commercial rivalry as a law of nature. To combat "anti-
social tendencies," to develop the "nobler side of
democracy," to assist in raising men to the stature of
manhood and to unite classes in the pursuit of higher
spiritual ideals became the aims of the Christian

Socialist group who gathered under the leadership of Frederick Denison Maurice in the fateful spring of 1848 and six years later opened the London Working Men's College. The scheme developed gradually out of the failure of experiments in economic co-operation which had brought them in touch with working class representatives and convinced them that the social problem was at root a problem of education. They were University men, and pioneers in a movement which brought the Universities into closer connexion with the life of the people. Some of them had lectured at Mechanics' Institutes, and often in defining their aims they criticised the policy and practice of that earlier enterprise. The Institutes had been founded in science; the College, having its origin in a scheme of social service, was to be devoted primarily to "social, political, or…human studies." Its function, however, was not so much to instruct men in specific branches of knowledge —and, as it happened, political studies were not promoted with unvarying success—as to develop personality and to establish a "bond of intercourse" between mind and mind. The College was, in fact, to supply what the Institute lacked, to assert an intellectual ideal, to substitute for disconnected lectures a system of studies, in which different elements of liberal culture might be regarded as parts of an organic whole, and to unite students and teachers as fellow-members of a corporate body. Students were expected to become "parties to their own education," to express opinions and difficulties and to benefit their teachers by an interchange of thought. In this conception of college life there was no place for the motive of self-advancement as it was commonly interpreted. Indeed Maurice went so far in his mistrust of commercial incentives as to protest against the introduction of prizes and competitive examinations, thereby opposing the tendencies of the age and penetrating perhaps more deeply than his contemporaries into the meaning of adult education. The fellowship of man with man, working together in the pursuit of high ideals, would supply, he believed, not only what was essential to self-realisation but the most effective stimulus to their thoughts and energies.

The London College owes its present position to students and teachers who have preserved it through successive crises, establishing it by wise reforms on a permanent basis. With its strong corporate tradition, its careful methods of class-teaching and tuition carried on with the help of University graduates and old students of long experience, its scheme of education rising from elementary beginnings to courses of a University standard and offering both a wide choice of subjects and a stimulus to continuous study, and the facilities it provides for intercourse between students interested in different departments, it may well claim to have developed many essentials of a University training and to be a fitting memorial to its illustrious founders[1]. But though by this example and in other ways their ideals have influenced the course of adult education, it cannot be said that they were themselves satisfied with the progress of the movement, that it stirred the masses, or

---

[1] If in admitting vocational subjects it has departed from the founders' plan, the Universities, as Professor Dicey remarks, cannot throw stones.

that it took firm root in the country. Of some fourteen provincial Colleges[1] one only (at Leicester) has survived, the Ipswich College having closed in 1895 and the rest at some earlier date. In most cases, so far as we can judge from scanty records, they did not differ greatly in the effective part of their curriculum from the more efficient Mechanics' Institutes, though sometimes a much higher standard was reached in literary studies. They formed part of a network of institutions and evening classes, working often in union with the Society of Arts, which aimed at supplying elementary, scientific and general instruction to students of all ages above sixteen who lacked the advantages of a continuous school education. From 1870 onwards their functions were re-distributed to a large extent between municipal bodies, Polytechnics, Adult Schools and the University Extension movement which diffused over a wide area the forms of University teaching which the parent College owed to an exceptional body of volunteer teachers resident in London. At the same time the desire for fellowship and personal intercourse with working men found expression in new methods of social service. In 1872, the year of Maurice's death, Canon Barnett was appointed Vicar of St Jude's, Whitechapel. The men who gathered round him as pioneers of the first University Settlement were following in the steps of the Christian Socialists who had started with the idea of taking charge of a district. But

[1] Including the Sheffield People's College. The Morley Memorial College, London (1889), was a later movement, forming in some ways a link with the Polytechnics.

whereas in their case district-work had been a passing phase, with which the Working Men's College had little more than an historic connexion, the very notion of a settlement was inseparable from the claims of a particular neighbourhood. The educational system which developed at Toynbee Hall differed from that of the College in that it was built up more gradually by studying the interests of different groups and uniting them round a common centre, and in so far as the results were continually tested by experience of the social environment. The early settlers were filled with the spirit of discovery; and the multiplication of small societies and reading circles, as fresh groups of students discovered their interests, is one example of the contribution made by settlement work to recent types of adult education. Not less important were their efforts to encourage an appreciation of music, art, and drama, to restore a sense of beauty and gladness amid depressing surroundings, and to test in various ways the teaching of Canon Barnett that only the best things can atone for the worst. Toynbee Hall has no doubt gone further than most settlements in encouraging systematic study. It was governed from the outset by a principle expressed some years before in the vague but comfortable formula of a Christian Socialist—"Our Universities must become universal"; and as an experiment centre it filled an important place in the movement known as "University Extension."

The phrase, it appears, was first used in 1850 with special reference to a proposal to establish permanent teaching centres in the larger towns as one method of utilising University endowments and opening a career to talent. The complementary conception of a "peripatetic University" affording "systematic education of a University type" in liberal arts and sciences to "busy adults," as opposed to regular courses for an academic degree, was defined more clearly in 1871 when Professor James Stuart invited Cambridge to become responsible for extra-mural teaching. The distinction was not at once generally appreciated; and in any case one result of Extension lectures was to assist the formation of local University Colleges. These in turn, as they attained the status of Universities, and sometimes earlier, developed systems of Extension lecturing, though the main burden continued to fall on Cambridge, London and Oxford.

Courses of lectures, supplemented by classes and paper-work and followed by examinations, formed the basis of the scheme with which Cambridge started in 1873. In its systematic procedure and the breadth of its interests—the first-fruits of the scientific renaissance and a new phase of academic research—the movement differed from earlier experiments[1], as also in the circumstance that it was supported by articulate demand. The petitions which came from all quarters—from women's organisations, from trade-unionists and co-operative societies, from Mechanics' Institutes and important towns—identified its aims with a new and catholic conception of adult education; but while its

---

[1] *E.g.* the circuit-lectures attempted by the Yorkshire and other Unions of Institutes in the 'forties, and the valuable Gilchrist lectures which started in 1868.

influence has perhaps been most widely felt among the middle classes, circumstances attached from the outset a special interest to its effect on the masses. The progress of elementary education created new possibilities; and there was evidently a desire among adult artisans not to recommence their education at the stage where their schooling had been interrupted, but to study and discuss subjects which specially interested them. How far experience of life would make up for their lack of secondary education and even enable them to render a distinctive contribution to academic studies, was a question now to be investigated over a wide field and one to which a "consolatory answer" was promised. Certainly one of the features which distinguished the early phases of the movement was the impression of mutual recognition produced at different artisan centres from Tyneside to East London. Not only in such subjects as economics did lecturers appreciate the value of information derived from practical experience, but at a successful centre, as the course of study broadened out over fields of science and literature, they met continually with a responsive interest which neither they nor their hearers could find words to express. To most lecturers it was astonishing that men who could hardly spell should write weekly answers to questions in which they were evidently interested. Further acquaintance revealed unknown depths of sacrifice—cases in which students risked unemployment or loss of pay to attend the lectures, studied under serious disadvantages to keep pace with the course, and travelled miles on foot to the lecture room, returning again to burn the midnight oil.

Examples of this kind have recurred throughout the history of the movement, and have supported the opinion of a great administrator that the "number of real students" is "in direct proportion" to the standard of work exacted by the authorities. Towards the close of the century there were the same premonitions of a crisis in University Extension as in other branches of the educational system. The promise of its early years had not been fulfilled; among work-people no revival had occurred comparable to the movement in Tyneside which perished in the miners' strike of 1887; and in certain quarters there were signs that the demand for lectures had decreased, a symptom observed fifty years before by lecturers who visited the Mechanics' Institutes. While at Toynbee Hall the "centre of gravity had shifted" from Extension courses to reading parties, societies, and classes, elsewhere old supporters had been replaced by a new generation more critical of the views expressed by lecturers on history and economics and perhaps, in so far as their interest in such questions had developed, dissatisfied with the conditions of study which prevailed at ill-organised centres.

It was a recognised principle that lectures should be accompanied by classes in which the teaching might be amplified and points of detail discussed. The "class" had been devised for serious students; but, whether it was effectively organised or not, it was not commonly in practice the unit of organisation, the choice of subjects and teachers being determined by the demands of a larger audience who attended and financed the lectures. Attempts to obviate this anomaly, which hindered systematic and continuous study, may be traced in the Cambridge scheme of affiliated centres, the London certificate (afterwards diploma) courses, and the evolution of the Tutorial class. Ultimately it became a question of distinguishing two types of education; in other words, of supplementing the normal forms of University Extension by a new organisation of student groups. The controversy goes back to 1852 when James Hole criticised the system of lecturing in Mechanics' Institutes. "The best possible lecturing," he observed, "bears no relation to the previous acquisitions of the auditory. If a word or an illustration is unnoticed or misunderstood, an important link in the chain of reasoning may be wanting.... The most valuable lectures are those which partake of the nature of class-instruction." When University Extension offered a remedy by combining lectures with classes, the argument was carried a stage further. "Students," wrote Canon Barnett in 1887, "must have not only the directions of the professor, but the constant care of the tutor"; and by stretching this principle he reached the conception of a Tutorial class. If class-methods were superior to lecture-methods, why not eliminate the professor, leaving the tutor to instruct small groups of students? The first classes called "Tutorial" were started at Toynbee Hall in 1899; but "Tutorial classes" had been proposed by a correspondent writing to Professor Stuart in 1875 and, I take it, were foreshadowed in the Students' Associations attached to some centres. Take for example a group of colliers at Backworth (Tyneside) in the 'eighties; one of them attends an Extension course at a neighbouring village, returning with syllabus and notes to repeat the lecture; all write papers and meet to discuss the lecturer's comments, puzzling it out until the weakest member is enlightened: all that was needed to convert them into a Tutorial class was the presence of a tutor, and money to pay him.

Closely connected with the question of supply was the problem of organising the demand. The local centres were self-governing units; they were expected to form representative committees; and at "mixed centres" with an artisan population there was often a special sub-committee to attend to their interests. Several northern centres were financed and organised from time to time by Co-operative Societies. The task as yet unattempted was a permanent organisation of the demand covering the whole field of adult education and bringing the Universities into closer touch with popular movements which had developed during the last quarter of the century.

The first Trade Union and Co-operative Congresses came in the interval between the Reform Act of 1867 and the Education Act of 1870, a significant cluster of events to which the modern labour movement may trace its origin. If political changes supplied the nation with an argument for educating the democracy, the democracy in its turn had motives for demanding education. A career was being opened to the leaders as trade union officials and representatives on public bodies; interest in education as a means to social betterment was likely to increase as political opportunities were realised; and the success of an intricate network of labour organisations, which provided an informal training in self-government, depended on the efficiency and intelligence of their constituent members.

While trade unions gave periodical support to various demands for education, the Co-operators starting with a broad ideal of social reconstruction gradually evolved an educational policy. The conception of a "State within the State," the nucleus of a self-organised democracy including education among its corporate functions, was implied in the programme of the Rochdale Pioneers, who, by devoting a percentage of their profits to educational work, led the way in a movement which supplied many industrial towns with libraries, evening classes and other forms of scientific and general instruction. A clearer definition of policy was rendered possible by the union of societies in a national federation and necessitated by the growth of State and municipal enterprise. In 1885 a Central Education Committee was appointed which defined, as the special objects of "Co-operative education," firstly the training of co-operators and secondly the training of citizens, and foreshadowed a programme of classes including the study of co-operation, economics, and industrial and constitutional history. The same two-fold aim of developing a capacity for service within the movement and an active interest in public affairs inspired the propaganda of the Women's Co-operative Guild, founded in 1883. Though the work directed by the central Co-operative Committee made little progress before the close of the century, it was important that a working class movement should have pledged itself to an educational ideal, especially when it is remembered that the same minds were at work in different organisations and ideas passed from one to another. The Club and Institute Union had kindred aims, having been formed to promote centres of social intercourse, in the hope that education might develop as one of their functions; and like the Co-operative Union, though on a very different scale, it endeavoured through a central authority and district associations to stimulate interest in social questions. It is interesting also in another connexion; for among the plans suggested as early as 1863 was that of a residential College where Club members might study history, economics and literature, not as a means to self-advancement but in order that they might influence their fellows. It was the same motive of social service that led to the foundation of Ruskin College in 1899. By that time the problem of leadership was better understood, the study of civics had developed and it became possible to draw on the labour movement for support.

The educational significance of this and other social movements lay ultimately in their power of creating motives, of "reinforcing the desire for knowledge with a social impulse." From the habit of association there developed a new outlook on life, an interest in problems of human welfare, and—as is suggested by the example of a religious movement whose influence is to be explained by its success in interpreting popular demands —a tendency to organise students in self-governing groups with an effective say in the direction of their studies. The Adult Schools, an offshoot of the Sunday

School movement especially associated with the Society of Friends, were undergoing a gradual transformation during the latter years of the century. Originally philanthropic institutions where the poor might learn to write and to read the Bible, they were developing into societies for the study of Bible teaching in its bearing on the "deeper problems of life." As a broader interpretation of religious ideals gradually effaced the distinction between sacred and secular subjects, so the spirit of brotherhood which these ideals inspired expressed itself in the development of the school as a self-governing community; and where the democratic principle was carried out in the management of the school and its component groups, there was a tendency to change the method of teaching, the Bible Class being replaced in effect by a system of study circles with a joint meeting of their members to discuss the lesson. Examples might be cited from earlier history in which the element of free discussion had proved an incentive to more or less serious study, and the growth of organisations which in various degrees fostered an exchange of opinion on matters of common interest was one of the influences which at this time created an environment favourable to the coming revival.

The century closed with memorable events—an Act constituting the Board of Education, the foundation of Ruskin College and of the National Adult School Union, and (following a special inquiry into the educational work of the Co-operative movement) a meeting of Co-operators at Oxford to discuss an arrangement with the Extension Delegacy (1899). This was, I think, the first quasi-official conference between representatives of a working class movement and those of a University. It was the herald of the Workers' Educational Association.

## 1900 ONWARDS

The Association was founded in 1903, a year before the jubilee of the London Working Men's College; and after the lapse of half a century the story of adult education seems to return to the point from which it started. The defects of University Extension, its precarious finance and its partial success with the working classes, recalled superficially the failure of the Mechanics' Institutes. Popular leaders were repeating Lovett's appeal for an educated democracy, and were as conscious as he had been of the inadequacy of the training provided by democratic organisations. And the new movement was supported by arguments identical with those which had been used fifty years earlier. Once again men were reminded that "intellectual improvement" had not kept pace with "material progress," that having learned to read and write they must learn to think, and that the art of living was as important to the nation as the "science of production." But if the problem of adult education was as insistent as before, it was approached now under more favourable conditions. Educational resources had developed. In 1850 the old Universities were on the eve of reform; fifty years later their influence extended in all directions and provincial Colleges were developing into new Universities. In 1850 State assistance was a debateable project; since 1870 the growth of municipal systems of elementary and technical instruction had been accompanied by the spread of Public Libraries and an increasing attendance of adults at evening schools; and there is a sense in which the Acts of 1899 and 1902 may be described as the charter of adult education. The new administrative system gave promise of a more effective preparatory training during childhood and adolescence, and by extending the powers of central and local authorities placed them in a position to assist experiments and to take fuller cognizance of the needs of adult students. And while in the Universities and Education Authorities there was a potential source of supply, the means of stimulating a demand for education were found in a network of popular societies and organisations which enlisted the most active-minded of the industrial community. More important still, fifty years of voluntary effort had accumulated experience and created traditions. It had been realised that busy men would devote their scanty leisure to studies of no pecuniary value, actuated in some cases by social or political interests, in others by a love of knowledge for its own sake, that adult education is not merely a device to make amends for defective schooling, and that in its arrangements a full share of responsibility must be allowed to the student.

The primary aim of the W.E.A. was to bring about a closer connexion between Labour and the Universities, to prepare and organise a demand for University Extension and to interpret working class needs. Its objects were defined more broadly in the Revised Constitution of 1907 which described it as a "co-ordinating federation of working class and educational interests," formed for the purpose of ascertaining and stimulating the demand for higher education and arranging facilities in conjunction with "the Board of Education, Universities, Local Education Authorities and Educational Institutions." It was by that time entering into relations with public education authorities; duties had been delegated to district councils and local branches formed in industrial centres; and several hundreds of working class and educational organisations (rising to 2500 in 1914) had been affiliated to the movement. Since 1907 special attention has been directed to the education of women, and since 1910 to the development of work in rural areas. While the initial impulse came largely from supporters of the Co-operative movement which at different stages in its history had responded to University influence, the Association derived its strength from the union of various forces and the heritage of past efforts and ideals. Of the earliest branches some owed their origin to Co-operative Societies, others to Trades Councils and University Extension Committees, others to district committees and pioneer branches, and it was an essential part of their policy to utilise every channel through which a demand for education might express itself. Their aim was to unite various interests and gradually to realise the ideal of an educational guild or College which had wrought on the adult imagination for half a century.

It was foreseen that an organisation of the demand would assist in readapting the supply of education to popular needs. While branches of the W.E.A. aimed

commonly at supporting Extension courses, a significant feature in their programmes was the arrangement
of preparatory and supplementary classes under the
local authority, and it was noticed in the early reports
that class-work in some form predominated over other
modes of instruction. It has been seen that the tendency
to supplement lectures by class-teaching, which since
1850 had acquired a more prominent place in adult
education, was illustrated by the University Extension
movement, and now it was proposed, in fulfilment of
this tendency, to supplement courses designed primarily
for the general public by the organisation of special
tutorial teaching for small groups of serious students.
So far experiments in intensive study had been checked
by financial difficulties and by the absence of a student
organisation strong enough to guarantee an effective
demand and to co-operate with the Universities in
defining a general policy; and in studying the rise of
Tutorial classes it is important to emphasise the
simultaneous growth of the W.E.A. and of a public
administrative system which extended the possibilities
of financial assistance. Their relation to University
Extension is best illustrated by the revival at Rochdale,
where small supplementary classes were organised under
the local authority in connexion with Extension courses,
the decisive step being taken in 1907, when a group of
students, having pledged themselves to certain conditions of continuous study for two (soon extended to
three) years, applied to Oxford for a tutor. Here, as at
Longton, the Tutorial class appeared as an offshoot of
the ordinary Extension courses which its members

continued to attend, and which afforded instruction in supplementary subjects. On the other hand this new branch of extra-mural teaching has developed in its progress the characteristics of a separate system. It has absorbed to a great extent the attention of the new Universities and a large share of public assistance. In its administration the representative principle is extended from the local centre to the University authority by the formation of special Joint Committees including nominees of the W.E.A., while a central Advisory Committee forms a link between different Universities in this branch of their work. The Tutorial class at the same time tends to develop its own recruiting base in preparatory classes and, through the missionary zeal which inspires its students to volunteer as teachers, to become the pivot of a new system of adult education extending downwards from one-year classes, the more advanced of which approximate to the Tutorial class and receive Government grants, to reading and study circles, lecture courses, and single lectures.

The demand outruns the supply, and alongside of the teaching provided by Universities and public authorities there is an ever-widening field for voluntary enterprise. One of the more notable signs of educational revival is the perseverance with which hardworked men and women in all parts of the country, in addition to pursuing their own studies, devote what energy remains to the service of their fellows. A Tutorial class is not deemed successful unless it produces offspring. Students who have felt the attractions of knowledge become its missionaries and start circles in the societies and clubs with which they are connected, and the surplus energy of a town goes to help in organising the country districts. Moreover the W.E.A. has no monopoly of the forms of study it has helped to define; and while it co-operates with various societies in supplying the needs of their members, its growth is one sign of a reviving interest in education to which different movements have contributed by systematising their efforts and defining their aims. The network of voluntary organisations has developed continuously since the rise of the Mechanics' Institutes, but only in recent years has its power been realised. It is not merely that new combinations have arisen, that different political and religious bodies apply themselves more generally to adult education, that old institutions like the London Working Men's College have strengthened their councils by admitting representatives of working class federations, while the latter contribute financially to assist educational movements, but in one organisation after another there has been an effort to arrange programmes of study, to recruit and train a body of teachers, to provide literary materials for their guidance, and to draw closer the bonds which unite scattered groups of students as members of a guild. The most striking example is that of the Co-operative Union which with its central, sectional, and local "authorities" and ancillary organisations, its annual discussion at Congress, its educational officers, its programme and scheme of grants-in-aid, its arrangements for training teachers and its plans for a Co-operative College, displays every year a more startling resemblance to an ideal commonwealth, and even like the national State, its counterfeit, commenced during the war a further development of its educational system. And if Co-operators have applied themselves more thoroughly to the study of their own problems, a complementary process of expansion (no less characteristic of recent adult education) is seen in the progress of the Adult School movement, which during the present century has greatly developed the secular side of its education with special reference to social questions and extended its influence by means of educational settlements and by close co-operation with the W.E.A.

If State enterprise has not diminished voluntary service but diverted it into new channels, so has it in a sense redistributed voluntary expenditure. Individuals may not bear the cost of their instruction to the same extent as formerly, but the organisations which they maintain spend considerable sums on adult education; and without the financial support of Trade Unions and the Club and Co-operative movements, not to mention an unknown amount of saving and sacrifice on the part of individual students, one of the most interesting of recent developments would have little chance of success. I refer to the spread of residential institutions, such as Ruskin College, which in 1910 passed under the direct control of working class bodies, the Labour College founded in 1909 by a rebellious section, the Adult School settlement at Selly Oak (1909), to be followed by the Co-operative College for which a sum of £50,000 was voted at last year's Congress. While it is the tendency of these Colleges to develop "Extension" work by correspondence courses and "local" classes, opportunities for residential study are rapidly increasing through a widespread system of week-end schools lengthening out into summer and winter schools, sometimes of long duration, promoted chiefly by the W.E.A., the Co-operators, and the Adult School movement, which has created special facilities at its numerous guest-houses and hostels. It is impossible to say how far these experiments may have been suggested by the University Extension Summer Meetings and the recent Summer Schools for Tutorial class students; but there is an interesting analogy between the latter and (for example) the Co-operative Summer Schools, in so far as both act as a stimulus to the year's work at local centres and both may be described as the busy man's substitute for Collegiate training. Further, as the Co-operative Schools prepared the way for a Co-operative College, so the *Oxford Report* of 1908 which defined the policy of Tutorial classes regarded them as preparatory to residence at a University. The suggestion was not original (for in 1879 Professor Stuart had pictured a network of Extension centres sending up select students to the University), but it was accompanied in this case by an important proposal which induced Oxford to adapt the regulations for her Economics Diploma to the needs of a special class of students to whom the ordinary admission tests were unsuited. The Tutorial classes and Ruskin College by demonstrating the calibre of this class have helped to convert a more or less hypothetical into a practical issue, while experience has shown also that the question of their admission to the

Universities is part of a large problem of providing opportunities for advanced study and of training teachers for different grades of adult education, which admits of no simple solution.

The rest of the forms of adult education, and whatever else has been omitted from this short narrative, I "wish you rather to learn out of" the Interim and Final Reports of the Adult Education Committee "than to expect in this place an endless catolugue thereof."

IV

# ORGANISATION

THE SPHERES AND RELATIONS OF THE STATE, THE
UNIVERSITY, LOCAL EDUCATION AUTHORITIES
AND VOLUNTARY ORGANISATIONS

By ALBERT MANSBRIDGE

Chairman of the World Association for Adult Education

WORKING within the English community are numerous
organisations constructed for the purpose of assisting
the grown man and woman in their pursuit of education.
These organisations at present fall far short of supplying
the needs of the population, but through co-operation
they may develop in such a manner as to render unnecessary the creation of any new bodies, although some
of their joint efforts may result in the setting-up of new
machinery.

A rapid survey of the situation reveals a new willingness on the part of the State to subsidise organised efforts
in education and to supplement grants of money by the
assistance of specially selected and experienced advisers,
ordinarily called inspectors. It is contrary to the English
spirit to keep any organisation strictly within the narrow
limits of its nominal functions, and so the Board of
Education, though a grant-distributing body, strives in
answer to popular expectation, to become not merely a

repository of advice but a source of inspiration. The President of the Board is looked upon to-day both as a missionary for education and as a crusader on its behalf against the prejudice and meanness which would stunt its development.

In our decentralised system, the Local Education Authority is the natural complement of the Board, but, unlike that body, its business is to supply education, being enabled to do so by monies raised by means of rates from its area and by grants of money from the Treasury, administered in accordance with the regulations of the Board. It has the power to make grants itself for educational purposes to voluntary or other bodies and not infrequently does so. Thus a University Tutorial Class may, and often does, receive financial aid both from Board of Education and Local Education Authority[1]. There are abundant signs at the moment that L.E.A.'s as they are called, are increasingly alive to the importance of those forms of education, which have no professional objective, but which are concerned simply with the development of personality through recreation or study. It will be remembered that the Cockerton judgment of 1900 approved the action of the Auditors of the Local Government Board in disallowing items of money spent by the London School Board on education other than elementary; but the needs of the case were so obvious, that provisional powers were granted by Parliament, authorising expenditure upon

[1] This specific type of effort will be referred to frequently in this article. For a detailed description, reference should be made to the Essay on University Tutorial Classes, pp. 181 ff.

the education of adults; and these were renewed until the Act of 1902 was duly placed upon the Statute Book. For some time after the passing of the Act of 1902 the Local Education Authorities were almost exclusively concerned with instruction and training for professional and technical purposes, although this was largely due to the demands made upon them, rather than to indifference on their part to national needs. Not a few of them supported the University Extension work, through which Oxford and Cambridge made a real contribution to the development of learning among the people.

The Universities of England, both old and new, occupy a place of their own. They are neither statutory bodies nor voluntary organisations and are, at the moment, acting in co-operation with the Board of Education, Local Education Authorities, and voluntary bodies in establishing a system of extra-mural work among adult men and women, which promises to develop into an educational force of incalculable power.

This survey has revealed a state of affairs characteristically English. The refusal to delimit the functions of bodies too sharply is in the interest of progress and development. Rules and regulations in the hands of "officials" can easily and often do exert a stultifying influence. The absence of such restrictions in the realm of adult education helps to explain the remarkable expansion since the passing of the Act in 1902.

It is not proposed to deal with Scotland in the course of this article because that country presents entirely different problems. Organised voluntary educational work has not flourished there to the same extent as in

England. This is probably due in large measure to the comparative ease with which poor students have secured access to the Universities and also to the fact that the love of knowledge and argument is quite common. In other words the Scottish people have not found it necessary to develop new activities. But the fact remains that the Scottish people in the big towns, who are really desirous of facilities similar to those in England, have found the more complete organisation of the national system a hindrance and not a help. Even Mechanics' Institutes, though founded in Scotland one hundred years ago, achieved more power south of the Tweed than north of it.

As the lines along which the State, the Local Education Authority, the University, and voluntary organisations may work in the near future, are examined more closely, it will be necessary to try to realise all the time that no artificial barrier must be allowed to remain in the way of the legitimate desire of the people to pursue their education in their own way and with the aid of such bodies as they may deem most suitable for their reasonable purposes.

## VOLUNTARY ORGANISATIONS

There are a multiplicity of voluntary organisations dealing in some manner or other with adult education of a non-vocational or non-technical character. For the present purpose, however, the consideration of other than those which have developed into characteristic movements may be omitted. All that effort which is the normal concomitant of religious life may be passed over;

but it is necessary to recognise that a great deal of the best adult education finds both its inspiration and its power in the Church or Chapel, and, as will be seen later, claims have been made that, in its more organised forms, it shall be eligible to receive financial aid from the State. Mere party or propagandist effort adopting the methods of education need not be considered at this juncture; but there are manifestations of such attempts which cannot be passed over; moreover the dividing lines between propaganda and education are often by no means clear.

A consideration of prominent voluntary organisations will reveal the nature of the position.

There are now several Adult Colleges for men and women, of which all but one—the Labour College—are of a nature which would justify the payment of grants in aid by the Board of Education, or the Local Education Authority, provided the regulations permitted, as in some cases they do.

The Co-operative movement has developed a comprehensive educational system directed towards the formation of co-operative character and the development of a knowledge of co-operative technique and principles. It has so far supported this work out of its own resources, only inviting State aid when it has undertaken the provision of Evening Continuation Schools. It would seem likely that as the movement has a definite intention, it will not at present seek to co-operate with public bodies, but that its members will content themselves with sharing in those educational facilities which may be provided by Universities, Board of Education, Local

Education Authorities, and voluntary bodies acting in common.

To a less extent this is true of the Adult School movement, the whole effort of which is based upon the study of the "Life and Teaching of Jesus." But since its interpretation is unsectarian and because it has made use of ordinary educational methods, it is certain that it will strengthen its connection with public bodies. Moreover, it has not infrequently acted for the provision of Tutorial Classes in co-operation with Universities and Local Education Authorities.

The war has brought the Young Men's Christian Association into prominence and it would seem that, although the basis of the movement is definitely religious, its educational aim is frankly more general than that of the Adult School movement. In any case, it is proceeding rapidly and skilfully to make alliance with public bodies, especially in regard to village work.

All of these bodies which have been mentioned, with the exception of the Labour College, have some kind of connection with the Workers' Educational Association, which at one time aimed at co-ordinating them all into one force. For such a specific purpose as the development of University Tutorial Classes it has largely succeeded, but for the rest, it has tended to become one body just as the others are, although differing, in that it is supported by them as affiliated organisations.

## VOLUNTARY ASSOCIATIONS AND FREEDOM

It would be well to examine more closely some of the characteristics and problems of these various movements before considering their relation to Universities and statutory bodies. It is commonly held that freedom of study is secured in a voluntary body, but this is only the case if the principle of freedom be definitely cherished above all else. Bureaucracy, or its equivalent arises in voluntary bodies as easily as in any other type of organisation, and intolerance is more difficult to guard against. An educational association, which seems to have an immediate object, must be more careful to safeguard freedom than one which has a general direction. In the nature of things the spirit of a body with so direct an aim[1] as the Workers' Educational Association can only exist in freedom, as the result of overwhelming enthusiasm for education in the largest sense of the word. Such a body in these days is in danger of being regarded, by those who misinterpret the trend of events or who mistake the proper function of education, as being directly concerned with the political development, through the medium of a party, of the working class as such, rather than as being solely concerned with what is fundamentally more important —complete educational development. An idea of this sort drives freedom away. Or again, if people of one way of thinking, or even with the same fund of experience, tend to use a movement, it is difficult for a minority to venture enquiries without reserve, much more to

[1] To stimulate and to satisfy the demand of working men and women for education.

express divergent opinion or criticism; the result being that such a minority becomes inarticulate or drifts out of reach. The connection of the Workers' Educational Association, however, with Universities and statutory bodies is in itself a distinct safeguard of the interests of freedom.

Of the movements which stand apart from such connections, it cannot be maintained for one moment that they secure freedom of study and thought. The student indeed must admit by implication a specific point of view before he enters his name on the roll. The Labour College states that "working class education, in order to be impartial in the scientific sense of the word must be *independent* of all the conventional institutions of education, and in order to be independent its organisations must take a *partisan* form—the form of that class which can alone serve the advancement of social science, the science which can alone serve the advancement of that class[1]."

It is obvious that no one but a "class-conscious" student who is willing to accept at the outset certain dogmas (couched in pseudo-scientific language), would find opportunity for development in the Labour College, which however draws its direct financial support almost exclusively from the South Wales Miners' Federation and the National Union of Railwaymen[2]. The members of those Unions, who do not accept the dogmas and wish for freedom of study at a resident college, would have to turn, of necessity, to Ruskin College, or, better still, to the Universities themselves.

[1] Prospectus of Labour College, p. 6.
[2] £1599. 1s. 3d. from each of these in 1919.

For certain types of mind, however,. there is great advantage in the existence of educational effort based upon partisan or sectarian institutions. There are many who would not study at all without the desire to serve some sectional interest. Moreover, people like to go to classes amid surroundings and in an atmosphere congenial to them. These considerations account largely for the recommendation of the Committee of the Ministry of Reconstruction on Adult Education, to the effect that "the State should not refuse financial support to institutions, colleges, and classes merely on the ground that they have a particular 'atmosphere' or appeal specially to students of a particular type. All that it ought to ask is that they be concerned with serious study." The Report of this Committee defined the safeguards upon which the State should rely as:

1. The fulfilment of certain conditions as to regularity of attendance and work, etc.
2. Inspection to satisfy itself by direct evidence that the educational work is on a level which entitles it to public support.

The Committee obviously did not mean that the State should subsidise propaganda, but that the claims to State aid of good educational work should not be prejudiced because the classes were organised by a "partisan" body[1].

[1] There is precedent for giving grant aid to bodies carrying on general education, even though the bodies themselves are constructed for specifically sectional or sectarian purposes. Indeed grants to Voluntary Schools are a case in point. Grants have also been made to Co-operative Societies responsible for Evening Continuation School Classes. The fact that service

For example, a glance at the Labour College curriculum reveals the fact that English Grammar and Foreign Languages are taught. Such subjects conceivably need have no bias. Indeed the meticulous orthodoxy of a typical English Grammar syllabus used in connection with the College takes one back to the days when "parsing and analysis" were the normal accompaniments of elementary school routine.

It is not likely, however, that such bodies will seek to take advantage of the opening proposed, for the visits of an Inspector would be repugnant to their temperament; but in any case, at the moment there is not the least likelihood that the Board of Education would approve the expenditure of Local Education Authorities in this direction, if asked to do so. It is a readily recognised principle that an institution supported by public money should not merely be open to all, but constructed to meet the needs of all those who may reasonably be expected to seek to use it.

In spite of these practical difficulties, the recommendations referred to are not without value. They indicate a clear conception of the supreme importance of encouraging to the utmost those adults who for any legitimate purpose whatsoever desire to acquire knowledge and to secure training. Such adults are rightly regarded as a national asset. Ignorance and lack of training are to be exorcised at all costs—certainly at the cost of grants in aid.

grants are made to men studying in Theological Colleges seems to extend the theory, though the circumstances in this case are exceptional and only temporary.

As we have already seen, the Co-operative movement is not likely to invite State aid for its educational work. There is no need now for it to organise Continuation Schools as it did so successfully prior to the Act of 1902, although it may establish Works Schools for its junior employés to meet the provisions of the Act of 1918.

Ever since the movement realised its function as a great force for education in citizenship and had its realisation confirmed by a succession of great educators (among them being James Stuart, Arnold Toynbee and Arthur Acland), it has persisted in developing an efficient system. In this work it has never held aloof from the work of other educational bodies, nor does it intend to do so, although of late its appreciation of "co-operative atmosphere" is causing it to establish a multiplicity of self-contained institutions such as week-end and summer schools, culminating in a residential College. This, for a time—and perhaps quite rightly—has weakened its traditional connection with the Universities, but unless the idea of "class" becomes stronger, there is no danger of isolation, which, though often cherished by short-sighted people as a virtue, is a disease which saps the life of all true effort in education.

In 1900 the movement entered into definite and active alliance with the Oxford Delegacy for University Extension. Under the arrangement then made, teachers of Co-operative classes could submit themselves for examination and, if approved, would be recognised by the Delegacy—their students being regarded as members of the University Extension movement. A number of teachers were recognised in this way but gradually the scheme fell into disuse and its only value now is that it stands as indisputable evidence of the educational *bona fides* of Co-operators, and of the traditional open-mindedness of the Universities.

The question naturally arises as to the wisdom of these sectional efforts. As has been seen, adults like to study in familiar surroundings, and with the people with whom, for social and economic reasons, they have made common cause. The significance which must be attached to this outweighs the importance of the fact that Universities, and perhaps also Local Education Authorities, could provide better teaching, although few Co-operative educationalists would admit this to be true, inasmuch as they themselves have a large choice of first-class University graduates and experienced tutors for their own work.

The Young Men's Christian Association and the Young Women's Christian Association, largely owing to the work of Adult Schools and the W.E.A., found that they could not meet the needs of soldiers and war-workers, unless they included education among the various amenities of "hut" life; consequently they have developed an educational system which promises to be widespread. They intend to co-operate at all possible points with Local Education Authorities and the Board of Education and to attempt to base their developments in educational work upon the Universities, which have by far the largest representation upon the Committee to which the general direction of the work has been entrusted. The Y.W.C.A. has in one respect proceeded differently from the Y.M.C.A., in that it has devised and constructed a residential Working Women's College, which experience led it to regard as an essential institution. It is the latest addition to a number of experiments in colleges for working people, and the educational strength which the Y.W.C.A. can put into it makes the venture of more than ordinary interest.

Ruskin College, with both men's and women's departments, is already eligible for State grants, provided it gives the Board the same satisfaction so far as its financial position is concerned as it has already done with regard to its educational standard; and it and the Y.W.C.A. College may ultimately prove to be test institutions, upon the experience of which future Board of Education regulations will be based. The residential colleges founded in connection with the Adult School movement and the Society of Friends, as heretofore and particularly in the near future, may desire to keep themselves entirely independent; and the latter may do so, enabled by that combination of commercial ability and christianised public spirit for which the Friends have long been noted and honoured.

For the rest, the efforts of Adult Schools, both in regard to non-residential settlements (of which there are several) and to the classes which every one of the 1800 existing schools will try to project, will seek to find a place in the national system. The religious basis of the movement will be carefully preserved in the main meetings of the schools; and in the strength and inspiration of a Christian ideal, both men and women will go out, as in duty bound, to classes on general subjects of education. If the Adult Schools fulfil a tithe of their intentions, they will provide a stream of enthusiasm and desire for education, which will help materially to expand the national system. Exactly how and in what way it will fit into that system cannot be considered, until at least one other voluntary movement has been examined, and the exact position of the extra-mural work of Universities considered.

All the voluntary bodies so far referred to have received a great impulse from the example of the Workers' Educational Association; or perhaps it may be more exact to say that they began to expand and their experimental work to increase immediately after the Workers' Educational Association had demonstrated the soundness of certain methods and principles. There is no need to trace the connections in a detailed manner. As has been already noted, the Workers' Educational Association set out to co-ordinate both educational and working-class movements. In its early days it may have had a vague idea that its success would lie in creating one big national movement out of several;—in other words, in becoming the accepted educational instrument of Co-operators, Trade Unionists, and Adult School men; but if so, it was speedily disillusioned, for the immediate result achieved, and rightly so, was the stimulation of such bodies to proceed vigorously along the lines of their own specific ideals.

As for the Workers' Educational Association, it gathered strength from the loyalty shown to it by these movements; and in areas where they did not operate and for people whom they did not touch, it was thereby enabled to provide facilities of all kinds and degrees.

Most important of all, by the help of the members of those bodies it was able to devise and to demonstrate the most important experiment in adult education which our times have witnessed. The early registers of the University Tutorial Class movement are full of the names of men and women who were, and are, primarily interested in the development of education through Trade Union, Adult School, or Co-operative Society.

The Tutorial Class reveals historically the fusion of voluntary, University, and State effort in the clearest way, and consequently further reference will be made to it after a brief examination of the University position. There is no need to discuss the educational principles of the Workers' Educational Association; but it may be well to note that the movement was admirably constructed to deal with the statutory bodies, because it represented no sectional interests. Its whole purpose and meaning was summed up in its conception of education as a law of ordinary human life, manifesting itself in the right working of the body, mind, and spirit of man. In the insistence upon the search for knowledge and the necessity for training in the use of it, it found its contact with the national system of education.

## THE UNIVERSITIES

The place and purpose of the University in regard to the education of the ordinary adult citizen is not easy to define. It would seem at the first glance that such an institution should only be concerned with scholars who are able to live within its precincts or at least who have at some time done so; but even in so narrow a view, it is implicit that scholars should go out into the world in order to purify and enrich the common life by the exercise of the spirit and the dissemination of the knowledge so developed and acquired. The influence and teaching of University men must necessarily be a finer and better, or at the least a different, thing from that of other men, or the University stands condemned, so far as its practice is concerned. Obviously, however, truth, beauty, and knowledge need not be revealed with the same degree of intensity as in the University itself. All sorts and conditions of men go out from its courts to "serve God in Church and State." For the greater part, these can only continue to be connected with the University in a nominal way; but there are also those who will go out in the name and spirit of the University to describe in popular language the results of research in the various fields of knowledge, or to speak to quite ordinary people of the many things which concern the human mind. In this lies, not merely the justification of, but the necessity for, "University Extension" as it is called. There is yet another aspect of the matter. A University must send out its roots and branches. It can never be a close society. The day of patrons, so far as places of learning are concerned, is over: it is the morning of the day for "all the people." A University, if it would fulfil its mission, must so interpret itself as to gain the affection and support of the people generally. In other words, it must have a direct and practical interest in the education of adult citizens.

This does not mean that it should concern itself with the spread of elementary knowledge—unless indeed it could do so in a different manner from that within the power of any other body—but it does mean that it should take its part in the inspiration and training of those whose business it is to impart the elements of education, whether to children or adults.

In some measure at least, the Universities of Oxford and Cambridge have fulfilled these conditions, and consequently, in spite of a feeling of discontent aroused by their apparent acquiescence in the exclusion of many scholars who were poor and in the inclusion of many who were rich but who could never possibly become scholars, they have not alienated the working men and women of the community. These indeed turned to them naturally when they desired to make provision for their own higher education, because they recognised in them the sources of power in education. The Universities on their part took working people at their word and at their request arranged with them courses of study, which were on as high a level at least as those of their own honours schools. The story of this, however, is told elsewhere.

## THE UNIVERSITY TUTORIAL CLASS—AN ALLIANCE OF STATE, UNIVERSITY, LOCAL EDUCATION AUTHORITY AND VOLUNTARY EFFORT

As the result of voluntary effort men and women turned to the University. The University was in a mood to grant the request, but the financial support it could give, or rather felt it could give, having regard to insistent claims in other directions, was not sufficient to meet the needs of the case. The students were in the main poor. Consequently the natural thing to do was to

approach the Board of Education and the Local Education Authorities. Mainly owing to the far-sighted
interest of the late Sir Robert Morant, the Board of
Education responded at once, and by a reasonable scale
of grants increasing with the need, the financial position
of the classes was assured.

The classes were also aided in several instances by
Local Education Authorities, though the initiative in
control, having regard to the nature of the experiment,
proceeded necessarily from the students themselves.
This was justified by the fact that the educational line
they took was so high as to receive the immediate
approval of the three types of institution concerned with
supporting them. The visits of representatives of the
three bodies to the classes were received with cordial
welcome, because they frequently resulted in added
strength and information, and at least in the expression
of another and experienced point of view. The classes
were in spirit and in fact University classes and the
students regarded themselves as members, even though
remote, of the University itself. Their own particular
interests were looked after by experienced committees
of the Universities, to which working men and University men were appointed in equal proportions. The
fact that this was at the time the only instance in England
of a combination of voluntary effort with University,
Local Education Authority, and Board of Education, is
important. All the representative forces united without
difficulty or friction and in such a way as to justify the
permanence of the arrangement. In the proposed new
regulations of the Board of Education which have not

yet been formally adopted, the University Tutorial Class stands on its own basis, justified by the representation of the University upon the managing body[1]. All other classes seeking Government aid must do so through the Local Education Authority, which is henceforward to be the determining governing body.

Up to the present, voluntary associations have been able to approach the Board of Education direct for grant aid, although the Board generally regarded the approval of the Local Education Authority in the area in which the class was situated as a necessary condition for the payment of grants. Before proceeding to consider this further, it is necessary that the University Extension movement should receive some further consideration. The amount of State aid given to it has been small and except when classes have been arranged for and financed by the Local Education Authority, they have been instituted as a direct result of voluntary effort and have been under voluntary management. Prior to 1902 they were assisted by the Board of Education as courses forming a reasonable part of the training of pupil-teachers. So far there has been no authoritative proposal in regard to them and failing other provision, they will naturally come into the system as part and parcel of

---

[1] "The Board will be prepared to make special grants, subject to the requirements laid down in the present Chapter and in Chapter 1 of these Regulations, in aid of Part-time Courses in subjects of general as distinct from vocational education, given under the educational supervision either of a University or University College, acting directly or through a Committee or Delegacy, or of an educational body containing representatives of a University or University College, and constituted expressly for such supervision." Draft of Proposed Revised Regulations for Continuation, Technical and Art Courses in England and Wales, p. 22, Chap. VII. 88 (a).

the work of the Local Education Authority in co-operation with the Universities. If this happens on any large scale it is clear that University Extension will enter upon a new period of power. Its financial disabilities will largely disappear because it would seem that under the Act of 1918, this work, like other work would be eligible for the 50 per cent. deficiency grant from the State, thus throwing only half the cost on the Local Authority[1]. It is a matter of vital importance that this development of University Extension should take place, because there can be no better instrument for the spread of popular culture.

The lecture as an educational instrument must be kept in the highest possible state of efficiency by the

[1] *The Education Act*, 1918, 44 (2) and (3).

(2) Subject to the regulations made under the next succeeding sub-section, the total sums paid to a local education authority out of moneys provided by Parliament and the local taxation account in aid of elementary education or education other than elementary, as the case may be, shall not be less than one half of the net expenditure of the authority recognised by the Board of Education as expenditure in aid of which Parliamentary grants should be made to the authority, and if the total sums payable out of those moneys to an authority in any year fall short of one half of that expenditure, *there shall be paid by the Board of Education to that authority, out of moneys provided by Parliament, a deficiency grant equal to the amount of the deficiency, provided that a deficiency grant shall not be so paid as to make good to the authority any deductions made from a substantive grant.*

(3) The Board of Education may make regulations for the purpose of determining how the amount of any deficiency grant payable under this section shall be ascertained and paid, and those regulations shall, if the Treasury so direct, provide for the exclusion in the ascertainment of that amount of all or any sums paid by any Government department other than the Board of Education and of all or any expenditure which in the opinion of the Board of Education is attributable to a service in respect of which payments are made by a Government department other than the Board of Education.

Universities, and their action must, as far as possible, be conjoint with the Statutory bodies responsible for the development of adult education.

### THE PROPOSED ADULT EDUCATION JOINT COMMITTEE AND ITS RELATION TO THE LOCAL EDUCATION AUTHORITY

The formation of Local Education Authorities rendered it inevitable that they should, in the long run, be responsible for or participatory in all educational work within their area. It has been seen that the Board of Education has now proposed, as a new principle, to make no direct grants to classes organised by other bodies, except in the case of University Tutorial Classes. A difficulty arises from the fact that active voluntary bodies, while quite willing to place themselves under the Board of Education because they feel that their point of view will be readily admitted, are opposed to allowing any and every type of Local Education Authority to occupy the same position. It is, of course, well known from experience that some Educational Authorities are broad-minded and allow complete freedom to the classes within their area, while others seek to trammel them by mere officialism. Moreover experience has often proved that classes which flourished on a voluntary basis have wilted away when brought under the control or influence of the Local Education Authority. The obvious line of action would seem to be that all bodies interested in adult education, should bring all their strength to bear upon the formation of a strong and reasonable policy on the part of the Local Authority. The Committee on Adult Education of the Ministry of Reconstruction sought out a middle way and recommended that, "Local Education Authorities should, when practicable, combine to establish within the area they jointly cover, an Adult Education Joint Committee. This Committee should be required to co-opt representatives of Universities and of bodies engaged in organising non-vocational classes aided out of public funds. The Joint Committee would receive applications for the provision of adult classes and would form a panel of suitable lecturers from which teachers could be chosen for the classes provided." This recommendation is the fruit of experience, and is at the same time in harmony with the proposed regulations of the Board. It would preserve to voluntary organisations their freedom of initiative and action, would bring them into mutual co-operation, would ensure the sympathetic treatment of each class, and recognise the supreme authority of the Local Education Authority, which must have comprehensive powers or decline in influence and usefulness.

The Committee was careful to abstain from recommending the creation of a Joint Committee by one Local Education Authority acting alone, for to have done so would have had the effect of unduly limiting the supply of teachers and would have placed the whole matter too much under the control of one body, which might at any time develop obstructive characteristics. The principle of co-operation was recognised in the Act of 1918 which provided for the co-operation of the Local

Authorities and for the formation of Joint Committees[1].

Immediately after the passing of the Act and the publication of the Report of the Committee of the Ministry of Reconstruction a number of voluntary organisations met to consider their attitude towards the proposed Joint Committees. Their decisions are not yet made public but doubtless they will be communicated to the Board of Education, in order to obtain, if possible, the assistance, if not the directions, of that body before the Local Education Authorities are approached. In the meantime, at least one Technical College, acting under a Local Educational Authority, has instituted a Joint Committee of its own members and the representatives of voluntary organisations, and although this is not a Committee of the specific type recommended, yet its formation is due to the recognition of some of the principles involved.

If the construction of such Joint Committees be approved by the Board and objected to by Local Education Authorities, there is little doubt that great pressure will be exerted to induce the Board to revert to its former practice and resume direct relations with

[1] 6 (1). "For the purpose of performing any duty or exercising any power under the Education Acts, a council having powers under those Acts may enter into such arrangements as they think proper for co-operation or combination with any other council or councils having such powers, and any such arrangement may provide for the appointment of a joint committee or a joint body of managers, for the delegation to that committee or body of managers of any powers or duties of the councils (other than the power of raising a rate or borrowing money), for the proportion of contributions to be paid by each council, and for any other matters which appear necessary for carrying out the arrangement."

voluntary bodies. There is however little fear of any
such objection, for the nature and principles of adult
education are now generally understood.

## LOCAL EDUCATION AUTHORITIES AND
## TECHNICAL COLLEGES

So far the whole subject has been discussed from the
point of view of non-vocational studies. This was
necessary, for there are no voluntary or extra-mural
University efforts concerned with technical training.
The provision for such has been almost entirely in the
hands of the Local Education Authorities themselves.
This is largely due to the fact that an official body is
much more competent to supply such education than a
voluntary organisation, and indeed the purposes which
justify the formation of the latter are not called into
question. Students who desire certificates and diplomas
in order to secure recognition in their trade or profession
are naturally amenable to the conditions laid down by ex-
amining bodies. They are in a mood not to question them
but rather to fulfil their conditions. Moreover technical
education involves not infrequently heavy expenditure
upon the purchase of apparatus and machinery, quite
beyond the reach of any ordinary voluntary organisation.

An immediate problem that lies before Local Education Authorities and Technical Colleges is how to set
on foot a system of education—both vocational and non-
vocational—which will enable men and women who
have leisure (and it seems likely that most working-men
will have an abundance of it) to study, not for advancement in their trade, but for the exercise and develop-

ment of their own diverse gifts. This will require an entirely new attitude towards technical education and it may be that, for its development, the services of a voluntary body will be necessary. There was an attempt to establish such a body, made some time ago, by the veteran Trade Unionist, Robert Applegarth, but it lapsed. In our system of adult education every student ought to have full opportunity for study, whether he wishes to learn about the principles of sanitation or the laws of economics; whether he wants to know how to bind a book or to write one; to frame a picture or to paint one. The tendency to exalt exclusively humane education has been unduly emphasised in certain circles of late, and all such artificial distinctions ought to be abrogated. Aptitude ought to be considered, not convention.

## CONCLUSION

The work of the voluntary organisations is revealed clearly as work of a pioneer nature. Those who perceive a new need are as a rule a little in advance of their time. It is for them to come together and to demonstrate both the need and the way in which it can be met. If they do this successfully, the existing bodies, both official and unofficial, will take heed and alter their own practice. Gradually the action of the voluntary body in any specific direction will become unnecessary and its success will lie in the transference of methods and principles to the public organisations.

Largely owing to the work of the bodies mentioned in the course of this article, there are abundant signs that Local Education Authorities will become powerful and efficient sources of adult education—especially if they adopt the principle of the Joint Committee. If this happens, it would seem that the voluntary bodies will find, not a narrowed but a wider sphere of activity, for they will be recognised and made use of as the mouth-pieces of the people they represent. Moreover educational experiment is never-ending. A voluntary body which is alive will always be making discoveries and entering upon adventures, without which educational progress will be slow and circumscribed, and official bodies, however wisely they may enter upon their work, will lack stimulus and tend to sink into what is known as "official routine."

The hope of the future lies in the continued co-operation of State, University, Local Education Authority, and voluntary organisation, for it is in that co-operation that the glory of the past lies. There is no other country that has manifested such a spirit in the world of education. England owes a debt of gratitude to the voluntary organisations which sought co-operation, and to the official bodies which welcomed it.

At the present time, the duty of the State is, roughly speaking, to support and finance adult educational effort of an approved character—that of the University to examine and reveal every aspect of knowledge, truth and beauty—that of the Local Education Authority to see that no portion of its area be left untended and no demand for education without an answer; while the voluntary organisations should adventure and inspire; taking up causes whether hopeless or hopeful which are essential to the full life of man.

# V

# DEMOCRACY AND ADULT EDUCATION

## By J. H. B. MASTERMAN

### Rector of St Mary-le-Bow, London

THE recent extension of the franchise has entrusted the responsibility of citizenship to the vast majority of the adult population of this country. It is the last stage in the process by which Great Britain has gradually given a democratic basis to its political constitution. Democracy is a new experience in the political life of the world, for the democracies of the ancient world were aristocracies resting on a foundation of slavery. The assumption that every adult person is qualified for the responsibilities of citizenship is one that may easily be disputed by anyone who knows the educational standard to which a large proportion of the electors have attained. If their function were merely to choose the best man to represent them in Parliament, it would still be true that an uneducated body of electors would be wanting in the power of discernment needed for the task[1]. But in fact the general body of electors is asked

[1] "It is not the lack of goodwill that is to be feared. But goodwill without mental effort, without intelligent provision, is worse than ineffectual; it is a moral opiate. The real lack in our national history has been the lack of bold and clear thinking. We have been well-meaning, we have had good principles; where we have failed is in the courage and the foresight to carry out our principles into our corporate life." *Report on Adult Education*, p. 7.

to give its verdict not merely on alternative persons but on alternative policies. Many of the most intelligent artisans have gained their political education largely in the Trade Union movement, in which delegates are elected to support a policy approved by the local branches by which they are chosen, and the progress of democracy in this country has been steadily in the direction of limiting the discretion of elected representatives. Intricate questions of foreign policy, problems connected with the defence, commerce and government of the Empire, with industrial, and economic matters, will in future be submitted to the judgment of the whole body of citizens. How can we hope to provide for the whole adult population an education that shall fit them for deciding wisely on such weighty matters as these ?

But inadequate knowledge is not the only danger that menaces democracy. A nation influenced by right ideals might safely entrust to its elected representatives the task of giving to these ideals concrete expression in national and international life. But an uneducated people is in constant danger of being deluded by false ideals. It will respond to the appeal of self-interest, and judge political questions from the standpoint of the present, rather than from their larger aspect. In a word, it will lack imagination, and will prefer the astuteness of the noisy demagogue to the far-sighted wisdom of the true statesman. Those who have come into close contact with working-class organisations have recognised as one of the greatest hindrances to their success the distrust that a large section of the rank and file of the members show towards their leaders. The only remedy for this distrust lies in the development of education. For the purpose of education is not merely increase of knowledge— important as this is—but even more the training of character. An educated man is a man who has learnt to understand the larger aspect of things, and to recognise the relation of every political and social problem to the past and the future as well as to the present. An un-educated man is always suspicious of what he cannot understand, and is unreasonable, because his reason has never been trained. Life itself provides a certain measure of education for men who are willing to learn, but the mechanical and monotonous character of most of the work of the industrial world gives no adequate scope for the development of the mental faculties of the worker.

The development of an exaggerated class-conscious-ness constitutes another menace to democracy. Class distinctions are mainly economic in origin, but they tend to be accentuated by different standards of educa-tion. Many work-people resent the system that seems to treat higher education as "the luxury of the rich"; and, on the other hand, those of us who have been associated with the work of the Workers' Educational Association have found how class-consciousness dis-appears in the fellowship of common educational ideals. Next to religion, education is the greatest safeguard against the στάσις which Aristotle describes as the most dangerous disease to which political communities are liable.

As a political system, democracy is founded on the

belief that every adult citizen has some contribution of thought and experience to make to the public life of the community. It can only become effective, if the whole body of electors bring to the service of the State a capacity for intelligent judgment and a strong sense of public duty. Political responsibility has itself a high educational value, and the extension of the franchise has undoubtedly been one of the strongest influences that have awakened a demand for adult education[1]. "As democracy has passed from a system of political machinery into a practical influence in the daily life of society, it has awakened a consciousness of new powers and new responsibilities. Men and women who a generation ago would have accepted without criticism the first opinion offered them, desire now to use their own minds and to form an independent judgment. They seek education because they believe that without it they lack something of the dignity of human beings."

One of the most hopeful features of the movement for higher education is the fact that, generally speaking, emphasis is laid on social service rather than upon individual self-advancement. "The object of adult education is not merely to heighten the intellectual powers of individual students, but to lay the foundations of more intelligent citizenship and of a better social order."

[1] "In itself the desire to use education to strengthen and inform the civic spirit is a worthy one. That men and women should be conscious that they require knowledge to form an enlightened opinion upon public issues is at once evidence of mental receptivity and the best guarantee of sanity in public life. It will be agreed, we think, that it would be beneficial if that temper were more widely diffused among all classes, and that efforts which promote it deserve encouragement." *Report*, p. 59.

The chief argument for democracy is that it harmonises these two conceptions of the meaning of education by linking the desire for self-expression with the idea of public interest[1]. Unless the growing power of the State in all departments of life is balanced by the growing intelligence of the whole body of the citizens, democracy may prove to be what Carlyle called it—"a self-cancelling business."

The bearing of Adult Education on good citizenship is fully recognised in the Committee's Report. The main purpose of education is there stated to be "to fit a man for life, and therefore in a civilised community to fit him for his place as a member of that community." Adult education is therefore "a permanent national necessity, an inseparable aspect of citizenship, and therefore should be both universal and lifelong." The training of the adult citizen for the right use of his responsibilities can be achieved in part by specific teaching on citizenship, in part by that general development of the ideals of life that ought to be the aim of all education. The Report defines the two essentials for education in citizenship as (1) the development of an open habit of mind, clear-sighted and truth-loving, proof against sophisms, shibboleths, claptrap phrases, and cant, and (2) the possession of certain elementary information and essential facts about such main questions as the

---

[1] "The adult educational movement...rests on the twin principles of personal development and social service. It aims at satisfying the needs of the individual and at the attainment of new standards of citizenship and a better social order. In some cases the personal motive predominates. In perhaps the greater majority of cases the dynamic character of adult education is due to its social motive." *Report*, p. 168.

Empire, the relations between Capital and Labour, the relations between science and production, and other such subjects. It is doubtful whether specific teaching on citizenship can be usefully included in the already overcrowded curriculum of our elementary schools, though something can be, and is being done to develope habits of self-government and co-operation; and the teaching of history could be carried down to modern times, and linked with local institutions. In the future we may hope to find a place for more specific teaching on politics in our day continuation schools, but for the present generation at least there is urgent need for adult education in the nature and significance of political institutions, international relations, and other subjects bearing on the exercise of political responsibilities.

On the question of the subjects that should be taught, I cannot do better than quote the words of the Report:

The essence of democracy being not passive but active participation in citizenship, education in a democratic country must aim at fitting each individual progressively not only for his personal, domestic, and vocational duties, but, above all, for those duties of citizenship for which these earlier stages are training ground, that is, he must learn (*a*) what his nation is and what it stands for in its past history and literature, and what is its place among the other nations of the modern world; (*b*) what are his duties to it, from the elementary duties of sharing in its defence and submitting to its laws up to the duty of helping to maintain and even to elevate its standards and ideals; (*c*) the economic, political and international conditions on which his nation's efficiency and well-being depend; its relation to the other constituent parts of the Commonwealth of British nations called the Empire, and the degree to which it can now or in the future enter into closer relations with other civilized nations for the just

treatment of less developed races, for the furtherance of international co-operation in science, medicine, law, commerce, arts,
and for the increasing establishment of world-peace (*Report*, p.4).

It is obvious that any attempt to deal adequately with
such subjects as these would involve the invasion by
education of spheres generally regarded as the monopoly
of the political controversialist. But "controversial
subjects need not be approached in a spirit of controversy." "It seems to us," says the Report, "a
positive gain that topics, which are discussed with
partisan heat on the platform or in the press, should be
sifted at leisure by groups of students with the aid of
books and in an atmosphere of mutual criticism." The
best security against the introduction of unfair bias into
the teaching of political and economic subjects is in the
sense of moral responsibility that every right-minded
teacher feels. But impartiality may easily become a
"pose," it is neither possible nor desirable that a teacher
with strong convictions should feel obliged to suppress
them. A second security must therefore be provided,
as is the case in Tutorial Classes and University Extension Lectures, by affording the hearers adequate
facilities for questioning and criticism. A good teacher
will welcome the opportunity of hearing points of view,
often crudely expressed, that are the outcome of an
experience of life wholly different from his own.

In the past the education of the citizen has been left
to the press, and to the brief and superficial stimulus of
electoral contests. The importance of the press as an
instrument of political education can hardly be exaggerated. If it sometimes fails to fulfil this function

efficiently the fault is largely ours. In a long experience of University Extension lecturing, I have been very much impressed by the support given by the local newspapers to the movement. The reports of lectures given in these local papers are often admirable, and their correspondence columns are open freely to what are often valuable discussions of questions dealt with in the lectures. A closer co-operation between the Universities and the press would do much to wipe away the reproach that the newspapers do not rise to the standard of their opportunities.

Important as this specific education is, good citizenship is developed not only by knowledge but also by the creation of a certain tone and temper that is fostered by a wider education. An educated man is a man who has attained to a right estimate of the standards of value, who "approves things that are excellent."

Education has this special advantage over other forms of wealth that it "scattereth and yet increaseth." One of the discoveries, which the Workers' Educational Association has brought to many of those connected with it, is the degree to which a common desire for knowledge can bridge gulfs of class and creed, and awaken a sense of comradeship and mutual affection among students and teachers of the most diverse social and political antecedents. It is a hopeful fact that the range of subjects for which adult students are asking has been gradually widening. At first the demand was naturally for the subjects that bore most directly on industrial and political life. But literature, astronomy, and even music, now find their place among the subjects dealt with in Tutorial and other similar classes. I have given lectures on Shelley and Wordsworth to large gatherings of work-people, and found them keenly responsive. As the grinding pressure of material needs is lightened by a more adequate standard of wages, and better conditions of life, the desire to achieve a spiritual interpretation of life will grow stronger. And a spiritual interpretation of life is an essential element in good citizenship. Democracy will stand or fall not only by its success in developing the material welfare of the people, but even more by its success in fostering those ideals of fellow-ship and service without which material welfare is of little worth. Rightly understood, politics are the vehicle through which expression can be given to the Christian law, "Thou shalt love thy neighbour as thyself." The unfortunate accidents that have torn asunder the religious life of the nation have precluded the Churches from what, in happier circumstances, would have been their natural sphere of activity. Whatever may be the case in the future, we have to recognise that at present great masses of the people regard with suspicion any education that comes from an ecclesiastical source. Good citizenship cannot wait till this suspicion has been cleared away, and while every effort must be made to enlist the co-operation of the Churches in adult education, the whole task of achieving the spiritual significance of democracy cannot be left to them.

By what agencies, and in what way, is the education of the adult citizen to be supplied? It would not be desirable, even if it were possible, for the State to provide such education, for the Elizabethan habit of "tuning the pulpits" would inevitably reproduce itself in the "tuning" of the lecture-rooms. Anyone who knows anything of German adult education knows how the control of higher education by the Government helped to prepare the way for the colossal disaster in which the German imperial system has gone down.

Still less must the education of the adult citizen be left exclusively to party organisations, which inevitably accentuate the point of view that they exist to promote. "As a constitution becomes increasingly democratic in character, the citizen comes to need more of the qualities of the ruler. On this point his education has been lamentably neglected. He has been taught, and well taught, how to present his own side of the question; how to discover his grievances, how to state them, how to press for their remedy. But he has not been taught how to see anything besides; he has not been indoctrinated with those wider interests, without the recognition of which democracy will be a danger to the world as much as a Prussian military caste[1]." It is both inevitable and desirable that citizens who hold the same political views should associate in organised efforts to convert other electors to the same opinions; but unless the electors to whom the appeals are directed have in some measure attained to the power of discrimination and disinterested desire for the public welfare which education of the right kind can give, the appeals of political partizanship will be grounded on prejudice and self-interest. What we need is some body able to guarantee the competence and impartiality of the teachers that it supplies, which

[1] *Democracy at the Cross Roads*, M. D. Petre.

can offer education free from the taint of patronage, and
which has no interest to serve but the public good. These
conditions are fulfilled by our English Universities, and
in a special degree by the ancient Universities of Oxford
and Cambridge.

An age-long tradition associates these older Universities with public service "both in Church and State,"
and while the new Universities may be expected to
provide adult education in their own neighbourhood,
their supply of available teachers is too limited to allow
of their doing more than this. But if adult education is
to be, as the Report claims, "universal and lifelong,"
the task that lies before the Universities is vastly greater
than has even yet been recognised. The burden of
finance must necessarily fall chiefly on local and central
funds, as the resources of the Universities would be
hopelessly inadequate for extra-mural work on the scale
that would be required. But the provision of teachers
would be the special task of the Universities, and a new
avenue of public service would thus be opened to a very
large number of the younger graduates. Oxford and
Cambridge have the opportunity of developing a great
missionary organisation, the aim of which shall be to
bring education within reach of the whole body of adult
citizens. The training of a great company of educational
missionaries will become one of the most important
departments of their work.

The work of adult education must offer a career to
men and women not less attractive than that offered in
the Civil Service. "If an adequate supply of teachers
is to be attracted, and if the work itself is to be per-

formed efficiently, the status, prospects and emoluments of the teacher must be such as to compare favourably with other work open to men and women of the required capacity." The training of such teachers must include not only the subjects that they are to teach, but also the art of presenting these subjects in such a way as to interest and guide audiences unaccustomed to intellectual effort. It is probably true that a good lecturer is born, not made; but the art of holding an audience is one that can be acquired by the right kind of preparation.

It is hardly likely that the Universities will be able to supply enough teachers to provide for the needs of the whole adult population. The educational "priesthood" must be supplemented by a "lay ministry," and the training of this lay ministry will form an important part of the work of the University-trained teachers. The experience of Tutorial Classes has shown that students, who have realised the enrichment of life that education brings, often become missionaries in their turn, giving to others what they themselves have received.

In this connexion, it is important to understand the attitude of the workers as a body towards the old Universities. In mediaeval times the "poor scholar" was as characteristic a feature of Oxford and Cambridge as he has never ceased to be of the Scottish Universities. During the latter part of the seventeenth century the social standard of these Universities gradually changed, and they came to be regarded as institutions for the education of the "gentry" for those professions for which they had a natural right to supply recruits. The

Universities were identified in the minds of the workers with the existing social and economic order, and it is only in recent years, that the feeling of distrust, and even of hostility, has begun to give place to a new recognition of the possibility of an *entente cordiale* between the Universities and the ideals of democracy. What labour is now asking is that the Universities should be open to all who show that they are able to profit by the educational opportunity that they offer. This demand may be met by a direct subvention, or by a great increase in the number of scholarships offered by public authorities. It will probably involve either a change in the social traditions of College life, or a great extension of the non-collegiate system. This is the most important question that will have to be considered by the Royal Commission that has recently been constituted. It affects the problem of adult education, for the Universities cannot hope to carry this on successfully unless they can win the confidence of the workers.

By what methods is adult education to be given? In the Report much attention is rightly directed to the Tutorial Class, as the most notable recent development of this department of education. But the Tutorial Class is an intensive method that cannot meet the needs of the general body of citizens. It provides, and will in increasing degree provide, a training-ground for men and women who will be able to stimulate and guide others in their search for knowledge. The University Extension Movement offers a less intensive form of education to a much wider community. It is not only a valuable recruiting-ground for more intensive forms of education; it is also a means of drawing together large bodies of students in a common desire for knowledge. In the effort to lay stress on the importance of class-work, the Report has failed to recognise the importance of lectures, especially if followed by discussion, in stimulating a desire for reading, and supplying information of real value. A course of lectures on Modern European History, or on Political Institutions or Economic History, may give to a large number of citizens a new insight into the significance of the problems with which, as electors, they have to deal. If rightly given, they present the facts from the standpoint of public duty rather than of self-interest, and show how the constitution of human society rests ultimately on the moral character of the individuals composing it.

It will perhaps be said that the University Extension Movement has failed to achieve all that its earlier promoters hoped from it. In some measure this is true, but it must be remembered that some at least of the causes that have hindered its success are likely to disappear. Shorter hours of work will in the future afford more leisure for working people, who constitute the bulk of the citizens in a democratic country, and better conditions of life will make reading less difficult. The growing recognition by Local Authorities of the provision of adult education as a part of their duty will help to solve the financial problem, and obviate the need of depending on the contributions of voluntary benevolence for the discharge of a public duty. There is no reason why courses of lectures given by accredited University teachers should not form part of the educational system of every town in England, and even of our larger villages. Such courses should be closely linked with the work of the local Public Library, and small discussion-groups would naturally grow up in connexion with them.

The recent awakening of political consciousness among women offers a specially hopeful opportunity for lectures by competent women on the political and social questions with which women are most closely concerned. Such lectures need not be limited to domestic concerns; questions of foreign policy, the problems of the Empire, the structure of political institutions, are all matters in which the woman-voter is beginning to interest herself. The chief reason for suggesting separate courses for them is that the times at which men are free are not always those at which women are most at leisure.

The provision of opportunities of education for married women is of special importance, because the nature of the work at home tends to restrict their out-look, and makes any kind of systematic study extremely difficult. Yet the earliest lessons in the significance of citizenship ought to be learnt at home, and as children grow up, a mother who has long since "forgotten all that she learnt" will be unable to respond to the call of their intellectual interests. The extension of the franchise to all qualified women over twenty-one years of age will bring the responsibilities of citizenship to a very large number of young wives and mothers, and if they are to be a strength, not a weakness, to the political life of the nation, a determined effort must be made to cater for their special educational needs.

If such efforts to provide education in citizenship are to be successful, they must win the support of the great labour organisations in which a large proportion of the workers are enrolled. Trade Unions, Co-operative Societies and the great Friendly Societies are able to exercise a powerful influence over their members, and the ideals that they have set before themselves include that of good citizenship. While working for the material well-being of their members, they are alive to the importance of education as a factor in industrial progress. It is not to be expected, or desired, that they will abandon the propaganda work in which they are engaged, but any effort to develop a more intelligent political consciousness among the people ought to enlist their sympathy and help, if once their confidence can be secured.

This is the more important because neither the Universities nor the Local Authorities have at their disposal the machinery for persuading adults to take advantage of the educational opportunities that they provide. The success of University Extension Lectures or Tutorial Classes generally depends on the enthusiasm of a few earnest men and women who leaven the whole lump of partially apathetic citizens. The support of the local Trades Council or Co-operative Society may supply just the stimulus that turns failure into success. There is a real danger that courses of lectures or classes paid for by public authority may languish for lack of the support that must be secured for courses that have to pay their own way. The idea that education is part of the normal life of the adult citizen is as yet new and unfamiliar, and it is still an educational mission *in partibus infidelium* in which the supporters of adult education are engaged.

Voluntary organisations have also an important part to play in supplementing the more formal instruction provided by public authorities. "Study circles, discussion classes, conferences, courses of lectures, and activities of less systematic character are in varying ways valuable means of education. They may be carried on in adult schools, working men's clubs, or trade union branches; they are, in fact, facilities taken to the students in places where they are accustomed to assemble."

The education of the whole body of citizens in a more intelligent appreciation of their political responsibilities is only one part of the work that needs to be done. Until recently, the governing class in this country was recruited mainly from our Public Schools and Universities[1]. This is no longer the case, and if the connexion between political and University life is to be re-established, provision must be made for the training of those who look forward to a career of public service in the sphere of political life. It is not enough to plant institutions like Ruskin College in juxtaposition to the Universities; the men who are preparing themselves for political leadership must be incorporated in the actual life of the University, and share, in such measure as they are willing to do, in its traditions and concerns. In many

---

[1] "The public school and the university have been, in England, not the exclusive, but the normal training college of the statesman, while his family traditions and home-life have contributed other features of dignity and breeding to the completion of the type. All these circumstances have combined to produce the gentleman statesman, a very fine asset of our political life." *Democracy at the Cross Roads*, M. D. Petre.

cases, such men will be older than the normal under-graduate, and must be given a status more nearly resembling that of Advanced Students. They will have much to give as well as to gain[1]; their presence would help to keep University life in touch with the realities of the larger world; and they would, in many cases, be quick to respond to whatever is helpful and inspiring in the atmosphere of University life.

In considering the problem of adult education, attention is naturally directed in the first instance to the needs of the class that constitutes the great majority of the citizens of this country. But education would fail in its most important purpose if it fostered the development of class-consciousness. The idea that education is a process finished in youth or early manhood is not confined to any class in the community; and the kind of adult education that is needed as a stimulus to good citizenship has no distinctively class character. The particular subject that men and women are studying matters less than the fact that they are keeping their minds in healthy exercise, and developing the fellowship that grows out of common intellectual interests. One of the strongest arguments for leaving the task of providing opportunities for adult education to the Universities is that under their aegis men and women who differ in their social, industrial and religious status can meet on equal terms. Many adults of the upper and

[1] "Universities should find room for adult students whom circumstances have prevented from entering a University in their earlier years....Adult students of this kind would bring a valuable contribution to the intellectual and social life of Universities, and it is important that Universities should endeavour to meet their needs." *Report*, p. 102.

middle classes are content to live on their intellectual capital, and unless they can be induced to recognise that the man who has ceased to learn has ceased to live, they may lose the influence that legitimately belongs to them in the political life of the nation.

There is urgent need of a nobler conception of the meaning of political life. Politics have become so closely associated with appeals to self-interest and the intrigues of party antagonism that many men and women who have kept their intellectual interests alive are disposed to stand aside from the duties and responsibilities of citizenship. The proportion of middle class electors who trouble to vote at municipal or other local elections is disappointingly small, and affords evidence of a weakness in our educational system that must be corrected. The representative system of mediaeval England broke down largely through the tendency to evade political responsibility wherever possible, and students of the history of the later Roman Empire recognise the same tendency as one of the causes of the failure of the local administrative system of the Empire. The only effective remedy for this evil is in the close association of adult education with the idea of civic responsibility. Legitimate self-advancement, and the pleasure that is found in intellectual effort, are proper motives for adult education, but the motive of good citizenship needs to be added to lift it from an amusement to a duty. To all this it may be answered that books supply to the citizen all that he needs for the cultivation of his intellectual life. It is quite true that reading is one of the most important avenues of education, but most men need some external stimulus to induce them to take up a course of reading that requires any real mental effort. And oral education has also the advantage that it brings together adult citizens in the pursuit of a common interest. For education, like religion, is incomplete while it remains merely individualistic. Democracy demands of every citizen the subordination of individual to common interests; and the kind of education that will make democracy effective must give expression to the idea of fellowship. Education, in the words of the Report, is "the expression in one sphere of activity—that concerned with the training of mind and character—of the interests and ideals which dominate the rest."

There is perhaps a danger that those of us who are closely associated with the various organisations that are engaged in the work of adult education may fail to recognise how limited is the field that has as yet been covered. It must be sorrowfully admitted that it is only a small proportion of the people that is prepared to make the effort to educate itself for the responsibilities of citizenship. But the experience of the past has shown that, to some extent at least, supply must precede demand. We must not be too easily discouraged by the inadequate response that we shall often meet with. Nor must we be content to cater for the needs of a small section of men and women who are prepared to make considerable sacrifices for the sake of education. The idea that education is a preparation for adult life, instead of being a lifelong process of self-development, is still strongly entrenched in English life. The educational mission to which we are called needs faith and courage.

Our resources appear inadequate for so great a task, and
it sometimes seems as though the ship of democracy
may founder, before those on board have learned to be
an efficient crew instead of a body of discontented
passengers. If the great experiment of democracy is to
prove a success, it must rest on the twin foundations of
high moral idealism and alert political intelligence. An
educational system that supplies these is our greatest
need to-day.

# VI

# LABOUR AND ADULT EDUCATION

## By ARTHUR GREENWOOD

Joint Secretary of the Committee on Adult Education

"MANY members of the middle and upper classes are too badly educated for any sort of work, whilst very many poor people are splendidly educated in subjects which seldom figure in school curricula, such as horse-management, farming, fishing, machinery, traffic, making a little go a long way[1]." Stephen Reynolds and his friend were thinking rather of personal accomplishments. But it is true in another sense that working people are educated. The various working class organisations provide a medium for the development of social qualities. Mr G. D. H. Cole has recently said that "the trade union is the working class equivalent for the upper class public school and university"[2], though the union, whilst it is particularly important as an educational agency, is not the only "university" of Labour. Other organised activities have played, and still play, their part in the education of Labour. It is largely the education derived from membership of those organisations originating in working class needs which has won for Labour the position which it holds in the community to-day.

[1] *Seems So* by Reynolds and Woolley, Ch. xx.
[2] *Social Theory* by G. D. H. Cole, p. 2.

The development of an organised industrial and political Labour movement from the miserably poor and unorganised masses of a century ago, suffering from the effects of far-reaching and fundamental social and economic changes which they could not understand, and subjected to the domination of a brutal race of "masters" who had not learnt that power brought responsibilities, is one of the most remarkable chapters in the history of the last hundred years. No doubt, many forces have been at work to bring about this remarkable change in the status and power of the workers. The awakening social conscience revolted against the barbarities and degradation which the gospel of "each for himself and the devil take the hindmost" brought in its train, and a considerable volume of legislation dealing with health, housing, and industrial regulation provided at least some of the indispensable conditions of working class self-development. The extension of the franchise in 1867, 1884 and 1917 on the one hand, and the abolition of the combination laws and the subsequent trade union legislation on the other, gave the workers weapons with which to win their own salvation. The growth of a public system of compulsory education, and the inauguration of adult educational movements gave to Labour some measure of power to use more effectively the weapons which had been placed in its hands. In these various directions, the working class owes much to the sympathy and breadth of view of men and women in other sections of society, and justice must be done to the part which they have played in the abolition of the grosser evils of the nineteenth century.

Whilst it is impossible to estimate the relative strength of the various forces directed towards the amelioration of the conditions of working class life, it cannot be denied that, as the nineteenth century wore on and passed into the twentieth, the most powerful factors making for progress in the working classes were those organisations which had sprung out of their own experience. It is, of course, true that the churches, and particularly nonconformist bodies, were a source of inspiration and means of education to a large number of the rank and file of the population. But it is mainly to the trade unions, co-operative societies, friendly societies and similar agencies that we must look to see the process of adult education at work.

The trade union movement is primarily the creation of the manual workers. It owed its inauguration to the need of the workers for industrial self-protection. It has come to be an important instrument for the realisation of their aspirations. Trade unionism which for a time accepted the existing structure of industry now challenges its basic principles. In its early days it was satisfied to readjust conditions and relationships within the capitalist system; it is now working for fundamental changes in the system. In other words, the trade union movement has forsaken its defensive policy for one of offence. For a programme of amelioration, it has substituted a constructive policy. This remarkable movement owes its present position and its power to the workers themselves. It has on occasion received valuable help from sympathetic friends of other social grades; but it has been built up step by step by the efforts of its own

members. Its policy has developed and its outlook has
broadened, not so much under the influence of external
"culture" or the teachings of those outside the movement, but as the result of experience and discussion, and
the force of circumstances. The trade union movement
has been, and still is, an educational agency of considerable power. On the one hand, it has provided the workers
with opportunities for the exercise of their powers
and "political" qualities, developed the sense of
responsibility, and given the members experience in
administration. On the other hand, the common social
purpose for which men are associated in trade unions
presents complex problems which call for consideration.
This consideration they receive through formal and informal discussions, and through trade union journals
and the Labour press. In trade union circles there is a
considerable volume of continuous intellectual activity,
which takes the form of a critical analysis of the economic
system on the one hand, and the elaboration of a constructive policy on the other. It is true that large
numbers of trade unionists are but remotely affected by
this widespread discussion in the realms of social and
economic theory, and that the consideration these
problems receive is often fragmentary and desultory;
nevertheless, the trade union movement has generated a
real interest in social politics, and its activities, problems,
and difficulties have driven its members to the study of
those aspects of knowledge which bear upon trade
unionism and the relation of trade unions to society.
The trade union movement is, therefore, an important
educational agency, partly because its government and

administration educate the members "by doing"; and partly also through its influence, directly and indirectly, in stimulating the consideration and discussion of the broad range of political, social, and economic problems.

It is a movement which has been built up by the workers themselves, and it is now one of the essential forms of working class organisation, contributing power-fully to the welfare of Labour, and in return calling for loyalty and service. It is true that often such study and reflection as it has stimulated has been biased against the *status quo*, but the obvious retort is that politics and economics have been generally taught with a bias in favour of the *status quo*. But the place which the trade union now occupies in working class life and thought gives it a prestige which must be recognised; and it enjoys the confidence of the workers to a degree which no other type of organisation possesses. Hence the important part which the trade union movement must play in the work of adult education.

The co-operative movement and the friendly societies are also institutions which in different directions have contributed to the education of the mass of the people. The former has developed into a gigantic network of organisations doing distributive business on a consider-able scale, and carrying on the production of many staple commodities. It has evolved in response to working class needs, and in its growth has brought more and more people into contact with practical administration. It has from the beginning had its specifically educational side, and it is now on the eve of further developments. Perhaps no agency is doing more for the education of

8—2

the woman electorate than the Women's Co-operative Guilds. The co-operative movement is now a powerful influence in working class life, particularly in the urban centres of the country. Its entry into the political arena will add a new element to the existing currents of political thought, by its interpretation of the problems of the day in terms of the ideals of co-operation. It will therefore, both by the practice of co-operation and the dissemination of co-operative principles and ideals, contribute to the education of the people. The friendly societies have been concerned with the problem of mutual assistance and protection through co-operation. Again, these bodies have owed their success to the rank and file of the population, and with the development of their work has gone the education of their members.

It has been necessary to emphasise the importance of working class organisations for three reasons. In the first place, the growing power of Labour in the community is due mainly to the organised efforts of working people. Legislative measures have but prepared the ground. In recent years the workers have owed almost everything either to "direct action," so to say, or to the pressure which through their organisations they have been able to bring upon Governments. They have influenced national policy far more from outside than inside Parliament, and far more through the organisations they have devised and which they control than through the ballot box. The middle and upper classes have no such weapons, and it is consequently difficult for those who are outside the Labour movement to appreciate the place which, say, trade unions and co-operative societies occupy in working class life. The intelligent working man is as deeply attached to his union or co-operative society as those of a different social grade are to their public schools or universities. The various organisations, originating as means of defence against capitalism, have become the media for the realisation of working class ideals. Adult education, so far as the workers are concerned, depends upon the co-operation of these organisations. In no other way will the pursuit of knowledge be incorporated into the texture of working class life and activity.

Secondly, it is necessary to realise that a very large number of working people have received an education of a valuable kind through handling practical affairs in institutions and societies with a social purpose[1]. Formal study and class work are not a substitute for this "education by doing." What systematic education can do is to supplement the education which is gained by associative effort, and to give fuller opportunities for the development of the capacity, which the successful government and administration of voluntary working class organisations have proved to exist. In view of the influence and growing responsibilities of Labour organisations, the Labour movement is realising the need for a large extension of educational facilities, with a view to the better fulfilment of the purposes for which working class organisations exist. There is, therefore, a strong

[1] All co-operative effort is "educational" in the sense that it develops a corporate spirit; but a trade union or a co-operative society has clearly a more important influence on mind and character, because of the complexity of its problems and the number of points at which it comes into contact with other aspects of the life of the community, than, say, a football club.

reason for making the organisations of working people
the foundation of a system of adult education. The need
for education springs from a desire to supplement by
systematic study and reflection the knowledge and
experience gained in practical affairs. It is a sound
principle of education to make existing interests the
basis for serious study.

Thirdly, it is essential to grasp the fact that the
growing interest in the problems of society is not due
primarily to the press, or to books, or to the rise of a
compulsory system of education, though all these have
been contributing factors; it is an inevitable outcome
of the trade union and other similar movements. The
association of men and women for a social purpose is
itself an intellectual stimulus; and the tasks to which
these bodies set themselves have involved problems
requiring a constant reorientation of aim and policy,
and the consideration of questions stretching far beyond
the boundaries of particular organisations. One intellectual interest begets another. Study and reflection
overstep the artificial boundaries of "subjects." Trade
unionists, for example, stimulated to study the economic
problems which are constantly pressed on their attention by circumstances, find themselves driven further to
the study of history, political theory, and philosophy.
Such a transition is, of course, very desirable and in
harmony with the Labour ideal of an educated democracy.
It is also interesting to observe that organisations conceived for one purpose provide through membership of
them opportunities for men and women to pursue other
interests in common. The various "Clarion" choirs and

choirs of co-operative societies are a case in point.
Co-operative societies in their educational work include
far more than the study of co-operation. The W.E.A.,
which is largely composed of working class bodies, and
which carries on so much of its work through its appeal
to the members of affiliated bodies, is responsible for a
large volume of educational work but remotely connected with interests which originally led many of the
students to seek education. The wider aspects of education cannot be divorced from its more specialised
aspects, and the hope for a widely extended system of
humane education lies in building upon the social
impulses and interests resulting from co-operation for
common ends, rather than upon an appeal to individuals
*qua* individuals or an attempt to "corral" the human
atoms wandering through the world like lost spirits.

It is clear that, so far as Labour is concerned, we must
look to working class organisations for the development
of adult education, and we shall not look in vain; for a
tradition of education has already been established.
Popular movements have rarely lacked apostles of
education, and it would be difficult to find a time during
the last hundred years when within these movements
the lamp of education was not kept alight. It would be
idle to pretend that all men possess a keen desire for
knowledge and the will to attain it; but yet, here and
there, even under the most adverse circumstances there
have been groups of men who believed in and sought
after education. It is not necessary here to refer to the
spontaneous educational experiments of the nineteenth
century, to the educational activities arising from out-

side working class movements for the instruction of working people, or to the part played by chartism, trade unionism and the co-operative movement in the sphere of education[1]. With the opening of the twentieth century, adult education received a new impetus. The working people's colleges, the University Extension movement, the co-operative movement, and other agencies which had carried on educational work continuously for some time inspired new developments. The opening years of the twentieth century were marked by the rise of new universities, all of which had before the war embarked upon some amount of extra-mural educational work. The time was ripe for a development of adult education. A generation of compulsory education had begun to bear fruit, and working class organisations, no longer struggling for mere existence, had become an integral part of the background of working class life. They widened the outlook of the rank and file of their member-ship, awakened class consciousness, and by the challenge which they threw out to the existing social order, whetted the appetites of working men and women for a reasoned solution of the problems of society. It is not to be supposed that the whole mass of the people responded to the stimulus of these organisations, but it cannot be denied that the twentieth century has been a period of ferment created very largely by the developing aims of Labour associations. It was during this period that the political Labour movement sprang into

[1] See *Education and Social Movements*, 1700–1850, by A. E. Dobbs, Longmans, 1919, and Chapter 1 of the *Final Report of the Adult Education Committee*, Cmd. 321, 1919.

existence, not, be it remembered, under the leadership of middle class intellectuals as on the Continent, but by the act of the trade union movement. The Labour Party is an offshoot of the Trade Union Congress, and its establishment marked an important stage in the history of working class organisation. In the industrial field Labour became more articulate and more clearly conscious of its aims. The tacit acceptance of a badge of industrial inferiority gave way to the view that "industry exists for man, not man for industry" and that industry must be re-organised to assist and not to stifle the development of human personality. There emerged the idea of economic democracy, and the conception of the control of industry by the workers. The co-operative movement found itself inevitably drawn to new ventures, and to a wider range of activities until it embarked upon enterprises on a scale both at home and abroad comparable with the operations of the largest capitalist groups. The first two decades of the twentieth century have witnessed a revolution in working class thought. The war period threw into bolder relief changes which had well begun in the days of peace, and the time which has elapsed since the termination of hostilities has but strengthened the hold of the new ideas.

The ferment of the times had its educational side. Ruskin College was founded in 1899. The Workers' Educational Association came into existence in 1903. It convened at Oxford in 1907 the historic conference on working class education, which crystallised the demand made by Labour for education of university standing, and which put the Tutorial Class movement on a democratic basis. The secession of students from Ruskin College led to the foundation of the Central Labour College. The effect of the educational revival was also seen in the co-operative movement. "The appointment of a director of studies, the new educational programme promulgated by the Committee appointed in 1914 to survey the educational work of the movement, and the recent decision to establish a Co-operative College, are signs that co-operators realise the importance of adult education both to the success of co-operation and to the well-being of the community[1]." These manifestations of a new and real working class interest in adult education are a significant feature of the twentieth century.

They were accompanied by an increasing readiness on the part of the universities to make education more accessible. Many local education authorities assisted financially the tutorial class movement and other classes organised by the Workers' Educational Association. The Adult School movement received a new impetus, and was largely responsible for the establishment of Fircroft, a residential college for working men at Birmingham, whilst it had close relations with the educational settlements such as Swarthmore at Leeds and Beechcroft at Birkenhead.

Considerations of space forbid any attempt to outline the variety and scope of the educational work carried on by the Workers' Educational Association, Ruskin College, the Labour College and the Plebs League, and the co-operative movement. In spite of divergence of

[1] *Final Report of the Adult Education Committee*, p. 30.

policy and method between these different agencies, they possess a fundamental unity of aim and purpose. In one sense, indeed, the bodies engaged in working class education form a single movement, expressing a common ideal. Ruskin College and the Co-operative Union are both affiliated to the Workers' Educational Association, and share its general aims. The W.E.A. which consists of working class and educational bodies and individual members has focused the educational demands of the workers and formulated their policy. The Labour organisations affiliated to the Association include, besides those mentioned above, the Parliamentary Committee of the Trade Union Congress, the Working Men's Club and Institute Union as well as many trade union and co-operative bodies; and working men's clubs accounted in 1914 for over 1 500 out of the 2 500 organisations affiliated to the W.E.A. Many of the affiliated organisations, such, for example, as co-operative education committees, carry on their own educational work in their own way, but this does nothing to impair the essential unity of the educational policy of organised Labour. The Labour College and the Plebs League have, in the past, stood alone. Whilst the W.E.A. has accepted the principle of co-operation with universities and other educational institutions, the Labour College has conducted its own work under its own auspices, on the ground that places of higher education are part and parcel of the old order, and that their teaching is not independent, but merely an elaborate defence of the *status quo*.

Yet this divergence does not destroy the single

fundamental purpose which lies behind the educational activities of workers' organisations. This purpose springs from the impulses which have led to a demand for education. As the Adult Education Committee pointed out in their first Interim Report, "so far as the workers are concerned...they demand opportunities for education in the hope that the power which it brings will enable them to understand and help in the solution of the common problems of society. In many cases, therefore, their efforts to obtain education are specifically directed towards rendering themselves better fitted for the responsibilities of membership in political, industrial, and social organisations[1]." It is not possible to differentiate this motive from the desire for fuller personal development, for, in a sense, both motives are rooted in the claim for the recognition of human personality.

This foundation for adult education has been laid by the various working class organisations working for the advancement of the workers and the realisation of their ideals. It is a conception born of experience of the needs of Labour. The Labour College pursues the common purpose by one method, and the W.E.A., and bodies which think like it, by another. The differences between the two points of view have naturally been emphasised in the past, but there is hope that misunderstandings may be cleared away and a basis of agreement reached.

The common aim of the adult educational movement cannot be achieved by any cut and dried method. But there are certain principles of action which arise out of the earlier section of this chapter. It is because of the

[1] *Interim Report*, p. 3.

bearings of working class organisations upon the future development of adult education that I have devoted so much of my space to the consideration of the prominent place which the workers' own societies hold in their lives. They are the windows through which the worker looks out upon the world. They embody his experience, and they are the instruments by means of which he believes his ideals will largely be realised. Broadly speaking, adult education must be conducted in the spirit of these organisations and with their participation or full co-operation. It does not follow from this, however, that every working class body, whatever its function, should itself become an educational association or institution arranging and holding classes. Of course, some organisations, such as the co-operative movement, have an educational side for this purpose. Other bodies will prefer to combine with one another for the establishment of machinery for providing educational facilities. This has happened in the cases of the W.E.A. and the Labour College, though the latter is founded purely on a trade union basis, whilst the former is essentially a federation of working class and educational bodies. An interesting development is that of the establishment of the Workers' Educational Trade Union Committee. The scheme which is at work is at present confined to the Iron and Steel Trades Confederation. It is a recognition by a large trade union of the importance of making provision for the education of its members, and, at the same time, of the limitations of trade union machinery, taken by itself, for this purpose. In essence, the scheme is one by which the W.E.A., in co-operation with one of its affiliated organisations and through a committee on which the union is largely represented, is endeavouring to meet the educational needs of the members of the Confederation. A number of working class bodies do at present carry on education work under their own auspices, and such activity will doubtless develop, but it will tend to be confined to less elaborately organised and less systematic forms of education. Where more continuous work is desired, the tendency will be to make use of other agencies, and more especially of those with which they have intimate contact.

It is manifest that trade unions, working men's clubs and similar bodies are unlikely to take upon themselves the financial burden involved in any large scheme of educational provision, nor is it to be expected that they should. Whether they will be prepared to utilise the educational resources of universities and local education authorities depends upon the fulfilment of certain conditions, which are concerned in part with the nature of adult education.

"Adult Education differs from other aspects of education because of the greater sense of responsibility of the students, the motives which lie behind their desire for education, and the peculiar contribution which they bring to their studies—a contribution which is the result of their experience. In the case of young people, their education is necessarily controlled by others; in the case of technical education, the choice of subject and method of treatment are largely determined by the immediate end in view. But where adults are concerned, we are dealing with a different set of circumstances." [1]

---

[1] *The Education of the Citizen*, being a summary of the proposals of the Adult Education Committee, by Arthur Greenwood (W.E.A.), pp. 15 and 16.

Adult education is essentially co-operative in character and must be based upon democratic principles. In the first place, the workers, through their organisations, must be adequately represented on the bodies administering adult education. So far as University tutorial classes are concerned, Joint Committees have for some years been in operation. Normally, they consist, as to half, of representatives of universities, and, as to half, of workers' representatives, nominated by the Workers' Educational Association. Generally the district secretary of the W.E.A. is one of the joint secretaries of the Joint Committee, and in practice organises the tutorial classes. This method enables the representatives of organisations from which the students are mainly drawn to exercise an effective influence on policy and administration. Without the Joint Committees, the tutorial class movement might have enjoyed a transitory success, but it could not have won solid and continuous support from working people. An analogous arrangement will need to be made as regards Local Education Authorities if they are to take their due place in the national scheme of adult education. The Adult Education Committee of the Ministry of Reconstruction recognised the importance of development on these lines. "The great need," they say, "is to set up some machinery which will do for non-university education what Tutorial Classes Joint Committees have done for extra-mural university education[1]," and they suggest that two or more Local Education Authorities should co-operate to establish an

[1] *Final Report of the Adult Education Committee*, p. 164.

Adult Education Joint Committee. "It should be the duty of such a Committee to co-opt representatives (1) of bodies engaged in organising non-vocational classes aided out of public funds, and (2) of universities[1]." How far bodies of this kind will meet with the approval of working class organisations depends upon the functions which are accorded to them. These organisations will wish to retain their freedom, for example, to utilise the services of the tutors who have hitherto been engaged in their work (subject of course to satisfactory proof of fitness), and to hold classes in the places with which the students are familiar, and not necessarily in school buildings. They will wish to safeguard the adult classes they organise from over-regulation and to ensure the fullest freedom of self-organisation to the students. The proposed Adult Education Joint Committees will meet with many obstacles before they are established on sound lines. The greatest difficulty, however, will be to induce Local Education Authorities to realise that the Committees will be successful, only so far as they recognise the essential characteristics of adult education, and the fundamental importance of building upon the activities of voluntary organisations.

Secondly, adult classes must be self-governing communities. The tutor must be a person acceptable to the students. The course of study must be worked out in co-operation by the students and the teacher. The time and place of meeting and local arrangements of the class must be determined by the students. There must

[1] *Final Report of the Adult Education Committee*, p. 164. See also pp. 84 f. of this volume.

be freedom of teaching and of discussion. In general, the responsibility of the students for the conduct and success of the class must not be smothered by over-regulation.

Provided these conditions are fulfilled an enormous expansion of systematic adult education is possible, for working class bodies would be led to take an active interest in its development, and their membership would provide an almost unlimited supply of students. As working class organisations are now realising the necessity for adult education, their interest in the question will not be confined to an active support of systematic and formal study, carried on under regulations enabling classes to obtain financial assistance from public funds. There will arise out of the educational work carried out in conjunction with Universities and Local Education Authorities, a volume of less systematic educational activity on the one hand, and of more intensive work on the other, related to the problems of Labour organisations and working class life. Nor will the education be confined to those aspects of knowledge in which interest was first aroused by participation in the activities of some working class body. It will tend, as education inevitably tends, to become wider in its scope, with valuable results both to the organisations of the workers, and to the community as a whole.

Labour must work out on the basis of its peculiar experience and in accordance with its needs and ideals, its own approach to adult education. The organisation, administration and methods of adult education must be in harmony with what Labour has found to be good in its own associations. The problem is not how to get the articulate workers to absorb the culture of a higher social class, but how to enable them to evolve a culture of their own. It is not suggested that there will not be elements common to both. But what is needed is that Labour should enrich the world with a culture woven out of its own deep experience of life. The expansion of adult education will be of enormous assistance in the development of a coherent philosophy, and in its expression through new institutions and traditions and in new standards of value. For learning is to the organised workers, not a superficial accomplishment, but a means of interpreting more truly the purpose of organised Labour. The results of wider opportunities for education, therefore, will be reflected in more clearly conceived ideals, and in increased power to realise them.

It is not to be assumed that the education, which working class organisations will support, will be tendencious and biased. Rather will the articulate expression of working class experience be a corrective to our present knowledge and an exposure of many deeply-rooted prejudices and conventions. The intelligent worker dislikes shams as keenly as the "educated classes"; he prefers truth to falsehood, and will seek truth. What many people regard as defects in the working class mind due to a limited outlook and lack of knowledge are often the manifestations of a different outlook, and of knowledge, which other sections of society may not possess. The assumption, that organised Labour is stuffed full of prejudices and without knowledge, is as false as the assumption that people regarded as educated possess a wisdom which is untainted by error and prejudice. The workers have strong prejudices, and their interpretation of experience is often highly coloured by these prejudices; but it cannot be maintained in the light of the history of the modern educational movement that Labour's interest in education is merely to confirm and strengthen its prejudices, and that it will deliberately shut its ears to knowledge which would lead to a re-adjustment of its outlook and its attitude towards the problems of life and society. On the contrary, those organised workers who have taken an active part in developing interest in systematic education, and who are daily influencing the outlook of their fellow-workers, have a passionate belief in knowledge and truth, and the courage to follow where knowledge may lead them. They recognise with the Adult Education Committee that "the cure for the prejudices of partial knowledge and one-sided thought is more knowledge and thought"; and that education is the means by which error and prejudice can be eradicated. The final test of Labour ideals, they realise, will not be found in the vehemence with which they are preached, but only in the truth which they hold, and in the knowledge upon which they are based.

But the approach to knowledge, so far as organised Labour is concerned, will not necessarily be through the orthodox channels of learning. The seed of education must germinate in the atmosphere of working class movements. Its nourishment will be drawn from the soil out of which it springs. The thriving plant will then push its roots deep into the sub-soil of our common

civilisation and gain new strength for itself. I do not
wish to convey the impression that Labour has no need
of the services of scholars, or that it should ignore the
large body of tested knowledge, and despise the world's
store of art and literature. The reverse is indeed the
case; what I wish to emphasise is that there must be
true co-operation between Labour and learning for the
enrichment of both. If learning has much to bestow on
Labour, it is equally true that it has much to gain from
Labour. What Labour can give is its peculiar knowledge
and experience and its interpretation of history and of
society. But this contribution it can make only if it
gains free expression. Hence it is that adult education
must be developed in the closest connection with the
characteristic working class organisations, for they provide the native atmosphere in which alone the working
class mind and consciousness can grow to fulness.

# VII

# WOMEN AND ADULT EDUCATION

### By Mrs HUWS DAVIES

Member of the Committee on Adult Education

THE education of women was one of the battle-cries of Victorian England, but the women in question were a small and select circle—the chosen few, usually drawn from the middle classes, who were destined for some profession. To-day the call is to educate some thirteen million women; since the long-threatened day is at hand when the women electors will actually exceed the men, and upwards of thirteen million women will have in their hands political power, the large majority of them having little more book knowledge to guide their use of it than what they brought with them from the elementary school. Had not many of them a store of that wisdom which is gained from the hard facts of a working woman's life and not from books, the case would indeed be evil. But even as it is the problem is a vast one; for a sound knowledge as to the best position of the sink in a scullery, though perhaps as valuable an attainment as any that some men voters could boast of, is not sufficient equipment for a member of a democracy, which shall have the deciding voice in such questions as that which of late sent millions of men to their death.

The social and economic changes produced by the war
—the impossibility of marriage for so large a number of
young women of this generation, and their consequent
entry into the labour market, along with many who will
marry later and with others already married but forced
by the high cost of living to continue as wage-earners—
have only made more obvious something which had
been slowly coming for many decades. The granting of
the vote has revealed it and the problems which it
involves in all their magnitude. Educated public
opinion is anxious now to provide some intellectual
training for woman the voter, though it troubled little
when she needed such training only to develop her own
personality, and to fulfil her exacting task of mothering
and training the nation's children.

From the point of view of adult education women fall
largely into three classes. First there are the women
earning their own living in industry, who have few or
no home duties to exhaust their leisure time, and who
have had sufficient previous training to take advantage
of the educational facilities which are organised both for
men and women. Secondly come women of means and
leisure, both married and unmarried. Thirdly there are
the married women who are occupied entirely in
domestic work at home.

The first class—that of women in industry—is a large
and a growing one, but its educational problems do not
differ widely from those of men, which are dealt with
in other contributions to this volume. Every class,
or course of lectures, or summer school, or choir, or
debating society, has its quota of women members. In

some their numbers equal those of the men and in others they outnumber them. Of these women students some are amongst the keenest and ablest members of the class, and almost all who attend at all work with that almost over-conscientious fervour which is so characteristic of the "new broom." Such women are very generally found to be wage-earners but of course there are always amongst them home-workers who have no children, whose children are grown up, or who, for one reason or another, have more freedom than the average housewife. The most urgent need in this part of the field is to increase the numbers of those who have any interest in things of the mind. The few who follow any intellectual pursuit are an infinitesimal number in comparison with the many, whose wildest dreams would not admit the possibility of such an employment of their leisure time. That condition, however, is equally true of men and must be combated along the same lines. But on one point, as Mr Wells' *Ann Veronica* complained so bitterly, "a man scores always, everywhere." The male worker, except in rare cases, has, when his day's work is finished, no tale of domestic tasks awaiting him at home. But the married woman-worker has often a whole day's work to do at night, the bachelor girl must often cook and clean for herself, the daughter living at home can rarely spend an evening reading while her mother toils, and even the most favoured have tasks of personal washing and mending which would not fall to a man's lot. So that to some extent the die is loaded against the intellectual ambitions even of the woman in industry.

With the second class, the women who have leisure

to pursue further education, and money to pay for any
form of it which they desire, we need not deal at length.
It is a class which is rapidly decreasing. Women who
before the war could afford to employ at least one
servant, can do so no longer, or cannot obtain one even
if they wish. Women who used to employ a nurse for
their children, in addition to other service, cannot now
afford such a luxury. The result is that to the ranks of
the overworked wives and mothers of the working classes,
are now added the wives and mothers of the "new poor,"
whose lot in many cases is even harder, as their income
is often less and the social standard expected of them is
higher. It is not one of the least of the social problems
which confront us to-day that a girl earning £300 a year
(a figure quite frequently reached since the war by girls
in the early twenties) must usually choose between
celibacy, or marriage with a man earning little or no
more than herself, followed by a life of unassisted
domestic drudgery.

There is plenty of room for improvement in the
intellectual standard of the leisured woman. An organiser
of a society described as being for "girls of education
and leisure" once confessed sadly that her members
were possessed of more leisure than education; and an
examination of the novels read by well-dressed women
in railway carriages, or a glance at the many women's
"fashion" papers would lead to the same conclusion.
But great forces for improvement, such as the replacing
of the home governess or "finishing school" by the high
school, the influence, during the last fifteen years, of
work in the suffrage societies, the experience of all kinds

of war work, and the coming of the vote, are effecting a silent revolution. The foolish and frivolous will always be with us; but as a whole the leisured women of England are far better educated than were their mothers; their lives are fuller and their personalities more developed; and the forces which have created this change continue to operate with ever greater strength.

The forms of education which attract this class of woman are too varied and too unorganised to enumerate. University Extension courses attract many; in fact middle class women are said to compose almost the entire audience at afternoon lectures, and from half to three-quarters of it at evening lectures in many centres. In every town there are multifarious educational societies of one kind and another—literary, musical, artistic—and in all of them women of means and leisure will be found taking a leading part. The women's club is not yet a permanent feature of English social life as it is in America; in fact no such clubs exist outside a few great cities. But those that are in existence are usually the centre of much intellectual activity, and it seems quite probable that the women's club may gradually become as popular an institution in England as it is in America.

There remains then that great and largely unvoiced multitude of "women entirely employed in domestic work at home"—the wives and mothers of the vast majority of the country—including now the women of the lower-paid professional, as well as of the working, classes. These are the mates of the men of the nation, who make or mar their homes and lives. These are the mothers who bear and rear the nation's children and in whose hands lies the hope of the future; and incomparably the greatest problem in the field of adult education for women lies here.

It is a familiar story—the gradual growth of the cares and tasks of housekeeping and mothering until everything else is crowded out, and the woman, who took an interest in the happenings of the great world before her marriage, has no longer time to read more than the headings of a daily paper. No one who has not done it knows the intolerable strain of incessant and unrelieved domestic work, carried on, as it so largely is, in smoke-laden cities and in houses specially constructed to make every task as laborious as possible. The daily labour of cooking and making and mending, and the incessant, eternal struggle with dirt may indeed be kept by a resourceful and determined woman within limits, but when to these is added the care of little children, a woman is faced with a programme, into which it really seems humanly impossible to fit any sort of intellectual pursuit. Millions of women have found it so. Few would exchange the compensating joys of home and children for any other state, yet most of them pay the price of this compulsory narrowing of their lives. If the truth were admitted, is not the idea of "mother" in the mind of the growing boy or girl frequently that of a creature of infinite self-sacrifice, but also of one who can be expected to have little or no knowledge on the subjects talked of in the world outside, and who has often a very considerable tendency to irritability and to "nagging" about trifles? The most tragic feature is that such women know and sorrow over what they have missed; and the best of them will spare no effort to make up the deficiency if they have the slightest opportunity. It was the writer's lot at one time to organise classes and study circles of working women, largely from the members of such bodies as Adult Schools and Women's Co-operative Guilds. To most of these women it was already a considerable achievement to be attending a weekly meeting, and to do anything more or anything involving reading seemed impossible. Most arguments left them cold though a little wistful; but when it was suggested that ever so little study for themselves would help them to keep in touch with their boys and girls, who were receiving educational advantages, which they had missed, and growing daily further out of their reach, the appeal was always irresistible to many, and all over the room hands would go up for a class.

The problem then to which this paper mainly addresses itself is that of providing for the woman in the home some chance of keeping her mind alive. As things are the majority grow steadily duller of brain and more narrowed in their interests during the laborious years when their children are little; and by the time they are old enough to look to their mother for guidance in things of the mind she is unable to give it and they have to turn to others. It is no answer to retort that her compensations are many, and that no one else takes the same place in her children's hearts—the point is that it is such a one-sided place. The wives and mothers of a great race should not merely cook and clean and mend and nurse for their husbands and children. They should have been able to develop and maintain that keenness of brain and interest in things outside the home, which alone can preserve a real comradeship between husband and wife, and which is essential, if there is to be that friendship and community of interest between mother and children, which will save them so often from the wandering paths that lead to disaster.

How far then is there to-day any organised provision for the intellectual needs of such women and how many of them at present take advantage of it?

Of provision there is really very little, and what there is is mainly supplied by the various organisations whose names will already have appeared frequently in other essays in this volume. The Workers' Educational Association has always admitted women to all its classes, but of the rapidly-growing proportion of women students attending University tutorial classes[1] it must be remembered that few would belong to the type of woman of whom we have just been speaking. Nor was the Association long in discovering that if it wished to attract these women it must arrange special classes for them, partly because afternoon classes were more convenient for many of them, and partly because they felt themselves to be less well equipped than the men and were therefore shy of joining freely in discussion. It may be said here, that this has been the experience of several other organisations, though there is a good deal of difference of opinion among women as to the relative

[1] In 1917–18 of the 2856 students, 1014 were women, while the percentage of women students rose from 16·5 in 1912–13 to 39 in 1917–18, a rise partly due of course to war conditions.

value of studying with men or apart from them. Certainly, however, one of the chief objections to studying with them is that women never get a word in!

Another organisation which brings a large number of these home workers under educational influences is the Adult School Union, which has an approximate membership of about 30,000 women. The work done is generally of a somewhat elementary nature, consisting of "first half-hour talks" on some educational subject given before the weekly Bible lesson; but it brings in women of little education, who would be frightened at the idea of a formal class, but many of whom are, in the best schools of the Union, gradually led on to join study circles, and to attend residential "week-end schools."

The Women's Co-operative Guild is another organisation doing excellent work among the class whose special needs we are considering. It is one of the most powerful and well organised bodies of women in the country, and though its object is actually propagandist rather than educational, its propaganda has so educational a result, that it must certainly be regarded as a strong educational force among that large body of sturdy, solid British matrons of the better-paid working class from whom it is most largely recruited. Familiarity with its work and with that of organisations in the Labour and Trade Union movements reveals the striking intellectual development which comes from work on public bodies. These have, until recently, been a world in which women have taken little part, to their consequent loss, but of late years, particularly during the war, women have found places on public bodies to a much greater extent, and there have been many Committees (*e.g.* Local Food and Health Committees) which have been obliged to include representatives of working women. In these cases they have often been drawn from such bodies as the Women's Co-operative Guild, and the experience of public work, following on the keen interest in public affairs aroused previously in the Guild or the Trade Union, and added to a practical knowledge of life, has had a remarkable effect on a very considerable number of women. In these respects all that is said here of the work of the Women's Co-operative Guild is equally true of Women's Trade Union organisations and of Women's Sections of local Labour Parties.

The great part now played in adult education by "Summer Schools" (not now always held in the summer) will be familiar to readers of this volume. A considerable number of women, mainly wage-earners, attend the longer-period schools organised by the W.E.A. and other bodies, but an absence from home of a fortnight or more, and often even of a week, is very difficult for the housewife; and to meet her needs many organisations, particularly the Women's Co-operative Guild and the Adult School Union, have developed short residential schools lasting for two or three days, sometimes at the end and sometimes in the middle of the week. To leave home, even for so short a period, is very difficult, but some women find it easier to do that by getting a friend or relative to take their place, than to find time every week to attend a class. When it can be done, the resulting stimulus from pleasant country surroundings, the meeting of other keen students, the advantage of good teaching and an adequate supply of books is such that most women who have once had such an experience look back upon it as a red-letter period, and a milestone in their intellectual development.

Women who do these things are, it must be admitted, but a picked few. A form of organisation which has of recent years come into contact with far larger numbers of women is to be found in the "Schools for Mothers" and "Infant Welfare Centres," now so widely scattered all over the country. These very rarely attempt any definitely educational work, though a few organise discussions among their members on urgent public questions; but for the most uneducated woman it is already something to talk every week or fortnight with a doctor or skilled nurse and to be taught the principles of hygiene, and perhaps something of the natural laws that lie behind them. There is an unequalled opportunity in these Centres for doing much more for the mental development of the women who attend them; they should prove an excellent field for co-operation with such bodies as the Workers' Educational Association.

Another hopeful movement which seeks to reach the parents through the children is seen in the "Parents' Associations" now being developed in connection with some elementary schools. The headmaster or head-mistress invites the parents at intervals to a social gathering at which some member gives a short address describing, for instance, the scope of some subject studied by the children, and explaining how and why it is taught. A general discussion follows, and the meetings result, in many cases, in rousing new interests

in the minds of the parents, as well as in securing that
co-operation of home with school which is so necessary
to all real education.

Two movements of recent growth and apparently
great promise are the Women's Institutes and the Women
Citizens' Associations. The Women's Institute movement, whose object is "to improve conditions of rural
life," had its origins in Canada and only arose in this
country during the war. But the unique conditions
prevailing then, particularly with regard to food, were
favourable to its development. It now has many
hundreds of branches throughout the country. Here
again the object aimed at is not mainly educational: but
the Institutes are entirely self-governing; one of their
declared objects is to "provide a centre for educational
and social intercourse and for all local activities," and it
is probable that their educational side is already being
widely developed in some places.

The Women Citizens' Associations aim directly at
educating women for citizenship and are already very
active and influential in many places, both in their effect
upon public life, and in the education of their own
members.

Other organisations might be named which seek to
educate the home-keeping woman, but those named here
are the most important and the most influential.

Nothing has been said of the subjects which such
women elect to study, and any attempt at enumeration
would be lengthy, for their tastes are very catholic.
Simple courses in English history and literature are
first favourites. They are not usually so much drawn to

economic subjects as are their men-folk, but a course called "The History of the Home" given in several classes roused an interest in economic history which might have been lacking had it received that more awe-inspiring title. For it is essential to success in such teaching as this that the subject should be so chosen and presented as to be easily related to the women's lives and to proceed from things they already know. A forbidding title may ruin the prospects of a class. Child study, for instance, has proved a most attractive subject, and when the class was made up of mothers and of elementary teachers led to very valuable results of mutual understanding and co-operation; but if it had been labelled Child Psychology, the teachers would probably have far outnumbered the mothers.

One criticism that might be made of the lists of subjects studied is that they are too "bookish." This is generally the result of the direct choice of the women themselves, who declare that they have enough of "practical" affairs in the home and want something to give their minds an entire change. But in one "practical" channel there would certainly seem to be room for development. Many women, having seen fresh glimpses of the beauty of the world through, say, a class in literature, begin vaguely to desire beauty in their own homes and surroundings, but they cannot embody their vague aspirations in any concrete form, because they have had no training in form or colour and no opportunity for such training offers itself. It would probably come most easily in learning to design and beautify their own and their children's clothes. There has been much progress in the teaching of decorative stitchery in elementary schools in recent years, and it ought not to be difficult to extend the teaching to the mothers. The Educational Needlecraft Association has already proved the success that attends experiments in this direction, and if teaching of this kind could be given, for example, in the Infant Welfare centres, much might gradually be done to bring back colour and beauty into the homes and streets of the land.

One feature which would strike any close observer of educational movements among women is the extent to which the students in such purely educational organisations as the Workers' Educational Association are recruited from the members of propagandist bodies such as the Women's Co-operative Guild. The whole effect of the domestic woman's life is to make her severely practical. If she can spare any time at all for work outside her home, it usually goes in some direction which will have an effect upon her home life; and she is influenced by some organisation, which seeks her out, to take an interest in such questions as housing, or the food and milk supply. With the majority it ends there; but the keener few, and the few who, being keen, can also manage to find the free time, are faced with a host of challenging problems, and are so stung by their lack of intellectual equipment to deal with them that, in face of all difficulties, they seek some mental discipline to fit them for their task. The most hopeful method, therefore, of bringing women into touch with educational work is to seek them out in organisations to which they already belong. Leaflets advertising a study circle might be put into every door in a street and yield no result, while leaflets distributed at a meeting of a Women Citizens' Association might produce the nucleus of a class.

This leads to our second question; how many women of the type which we are considering take part at present in any sort of educational activity? The answer is that, compared with the whole, the number is infinitesimally small. Rows upon rows of streets, almost every house containing some woman for whom it is home and workshop, would yield only a very few who ever find their way to any of the societies which we have been considering, or ever go out at all, except to shop, or push the perambulator, or visit a friend, or, as a rare diversion, "see the pictures."

One reason, of course, is that early education has been so defective and so useless, as far as the majority are concerned, that there are few who really take any active interest in things of the mind, and this is true of both sexes and of every rank of life. Only the slow work of years can change that. But it is not the only cause which keeps serious classes and meetings of women few and small. Behind the closed doors in all those rows of streets are thousands of women whom no persuasion would bring to anything more mentally exacting than a cinema. Let us hope that their daughters, or at least their granddaughters, will be of another mind. But there are also hundreds of women, one here and one there, who yearn amid the eternal round of mops and pots and pans for something which would revive their mental life, and lift their ever-narrowing horizon. Often they do not know where to look for it, but often, when they do, they have regretfully to let it pass them by, because their difficulties are too great.

What are these difficulties? First and foremost comes the sheer physical inability to do more than they are already doing. Most of them live in houses so built and equipped, that every task is doubly or trebly more laborious than it need be. When one woman, under the conditions now prevailing, has to cook, clean, sew, wash, iron, and shop for a family of four or five, she may well smile wearily at the well-meant invitation to join a class in English literature. When she has a young baby crying in the background, she might almost be excused if she shut the door hastily in her kindly visitor's face. How, for instance, is the woman who gave this account of her domestic conditions to find time to join a class? (She was the wife and mother of miners who worked on the "three-shift" system):

John has his breakfast at 4.30 for the morning shift. When that is over I have to prepare breakfast for Will, who returns about 7 from the night shift. Then about 10 or 11 I have to get breakfast for Sam, who got home from the afternoon shift about 11 p.m. when of course he had to have his supper. The same thing goes on with each meal, and when you consider that there are the children to feed and get off to school by certain hours, you can imagine what this house is like. It is nothing more than an eating-house, and the back-kitchen is always a-swill with the men's baths.

The occupation of the woman working at home is unique in having no fixed hours, and generally no fixed pay! Her working hours are more nearly 84 than 48, and it may be noted, incidentally, that the 47 and 48

hour week for her men has only lengthened her day—
for whereas she used to put their cold breakfast ready
over-night for them to take with them, she now has to
get up and cook a hot one.  She may get snatches of
leisure at odd times; but it is hard to see how, under
prevailing conditions, she is to get that regular free
time weekly, which is essential if she is to join in any
organised education.  She cannot do it unless other
members of her family recognise her need for it, and
undertake her work at the time she wants to be free,
even if it be only to look after the children and prepare
the supper once a week.  Growing and grown-up
daughters are often, though by no means always, ready
to help in this way, but to husbands and sons it rarely
occurs.  In the servantless households of middle-class
people, particularly of the younger generation, there is
an increasing tendency for a man to help his wife as far
as he can with household tasks; but in working-class
families the idea seems to be largely unknown, and was,
indeed, greeted with amazed surprise by two distinguished Trade Union leaders in a discussion on the
subject. The Adult School Union, which seeks to reach
women as much as men, has always urged upon its men
members the necessity of helping their wives to be free
for their weekly school, and, simple and homely though
the idea may be, other bodies might do well to follow
the example, for the new social order can never come
while women lag intellectually far behind men.

Another cause holding back women from outside
interests is, with alarming frequency, ill-health.  Few
of those more fortunately placed realise how many

working women suffer from chronic bad health, very often due to over-work and to lack of skilled care and suitable conditions in maternity. The marvellous thing is that such women are able to perform their daily tasks at all, and to expect them to do anything but rest when their work is done would be futile. The remedy for the social conditions which largely create this particular problem lies with the Ministry of Health.

As has been suggested earlier many of the classes and meetings arranged for women have been held in the afternoon, because, with the morning's work done and the older children in school, that is a woman's freest time. But if she has quite young children she is still-tied, and many a teacher and speaker remembers the unhappy experience of trying to make her voice drown a baby's insistent and increasing cry, and assuring the distracted mother that she quite liked it. The mother usually failed to appear herself the following week. The nursery schools will, for those who desire it, relieve the mother of all but the babies, but it seems essential to the success of any educational effort among working-class women that, at the place of meeting, there should be a suitable room for the babies, with plenty of skilled care available. This has already been arranged by many organisations of all sorts, and it has contributed enormously to the success of their classes; for the mother has now the double attraction both of the class, and of a period of rest from her baby, while knowing that it is well cared for.

Before many domestic women can be lured into classes then, they must have better houses, equipped with all possible labour-saving appliances; their men must have better industrial conditions, and particularly baths at the place of work for miners and other men following grimy occupations; there must be better care and provision for the health of the mothers of the country, so that the years of child-bearing be not more burdensome than is inevitable; and there must be assistance, both on the part of her own family, and of the class she attends, to relieve the housewife of those tasks which cannot be put entirely aside even for a few hours.

But even if all these conditions were realised the organisers of a class for women might often be disappointed in the response, for women will not, any more than men, attend a class regularly unless its whole atmosphere is attractive to them. Many factors go to the creation of such an attraction—the subject, the teacher, the meeting-place, and the general spirit of friendliness among the members. After watching a good many experiments, some which have failed, and some which have succeeded, the writer would be inclined to say that nothing else is so essential as that the class should be genuinely independent and self-governing. The members should have unfettered choice as to subject, and be invited, as far as possible, to suggest the lines of study. It may not be feasible for them actually to select the teacher, but they should have the right of rejecting her (or him) should she prove unsuitable. In everything they must feel that it is *their* class, and that nothing can make and keep it successful except their own individual effort.

The personality of the teacher is of first importance
in all education, and it is none the less so in such work
as this. Assuming that the teacher is a woman (though
there is no reason why she should be) she must have a
sound academic knowledge of her subject; but she must
also have much tact, and wide sympathy, and knowledge
of the world, or she will never get into real touch with
the minds of her students. So important is a real understanding of their lives and minds, that there is a widespread desire for more opportunities to train the ablest
students so that they themselves may become class-
teachers. The University tutorial classes have done much
along this line; but there is great need of some more
concentrated training, which could only be supplied by
a residential college. When the war broke out there
were several schemes on foot for the founding of
working women's colleges, but most of them were
temporarily held up. A small experiment at Greenhow
(Cheshunt) remained in existence, and the Adult School
Union has had women in residence for periods of some
months at "Penscot," Shipham, Somerset, and at Ford
Cottage, York. Ruskin College has this year opened its
doors to women, and has a Women's Hostel with seven
students in residence now, and the prospect of a
considerably larger number in the autumn. The Young
Women's Christian Association has also founded a
working women's college at Beckenham, which has now
(March, 1920) 11 students. It is not suggested of course
that all, or even most, of the students in these colleges
will turn to teaching work, but many of them will; and
the colleges, which seem likely to spring up in connection

with various movements, will always be a channel to which the best brains in the movement can flow, returning again to enrich the whole. The number who can reach such colleges, even for short periods, can, perhaps, never be great; but there is no doubt that even short periods of residence are likely to produce greater results than years of study at home. The detachment from the cares of home life, and from the fatigue of the factory or workroom, the pleasant surroundings, the inspiration of good teaching, and the leisure to read and think, all combine to create a new world of the mind and spirit, and life will never be the same again to these women, even though they may return to the same round of work.

There is no doubt then that the field of women's education is ready, not yet for the harvest, but for the careful tending and fostering which shall yield the harvest. Fifty years of elementary education, the woman's movement of the last fifteen years, whose influence has reached even the most home-keeping woman, and finally the tremendous upheaval of the war, have created a demand which will grow steadily greater. The difficulties in the way are great, but here and there they are being so triumphantly met that we must believe that the same success would follow the right conditions everywhere.

Much hard and self-sacrificing work must be done before England achieves an educated womanhood, but the reward will be great. The day will yet come when elementary and continued education will awaken genuine and lasting interests which later life will not deaden, and when a race of women shall arise, who, still ministering to the health and comfort of husband and children, shall be the intellectual comrades of their husbands, and the friends to whom their children can bring all their questions, hopes and aspirations.

# VIII

## THE UNIVERSITY EXTENSION MOVEMENT

By Miss ALICE THOMPSON

Hon. Secretary of the Cambridge Local Lectures Union
and of the Scarborough centre

ONE of the most crying needs of the present day is undoubtedly that of a complete and well organised scheme of Adult Education.

It is becoming generally recognised that a preparation for life by education is not sufficient  there must also be a continuation of education throughout life, if a real and efficient citizenship is to be both secured and maintained.

The Report of the Adult Education Committee dwells in detail on these facts.

It records the needs as vital, the desires of the community as urgent; it tabulates and describes the agencies in active work and dwells on future possibilities, emphasising clearly that Adult Education must be regarded no longer as a luxury, but as an essential to life and progress.

It is the object of this essay to examine as fully as possible the character and position of one of these agencies—University Extension—to consider its origin and development, its present position, and the great possibilities which are in store for it, if only it can be true to its traditions, and can receive that public recognition which is of vital importance.

There can be no doubt to anyone who weighs carefully our national history and characteristics, that no official, cut and dried, universal scheme of Adult Education could ever succeed. It would be opposed to all tradition and to our best instincts. At the same time, our often haphazard method of procedure wastes both effort, time, and money and tends to inefficiency. The interests of education seem now to demand a well thought out co-ordination of all existing agencies, voluntary and otherwise, and an earnest and sympathetic co-operation between them, with whatever State initiative, assistance, and supervision appears necessary.

Both the Education Act of 1918 and the Adult Education Report recognise this and it is therefore of great importance that each organisation should be fully examined and tested.

The chief existing agencies for Adult Education may be summarised as Working-men's Colleges, University Extension Lectures, the Tutorial Class System of the Workers' Educational Association, Settlements, the work of Co-operative Societies and the rapidly expanding work of the Y.M.C.A. It can be clearly shown that University Extension holds a definite and unique position in the category and should form a vital part of the organism which we desire to see evolved.

In weighing the merits and claims of any institution, it is of the highest importance to consider, in the first place, its aims and ideals, whether it has fallen short of their attainment or not; for therein lies its strength.

> " It is not what man does that exalts him,
> But what man would do,"

Browning reminds us.

What then were the origin of the University Extension movement and the ideals of its founders?

There can be no doubt, that, like every other great development, the prophet and the dreamer, the ''men before their time," had an intimate share. We recall the desires of the middle of the last century, that the Universities should become truly national; and as Mark Pattison truly said, ''The ideal of a national University is that it should be co-extensive with the nation; it should be the common source of the whole of the higher (or secondary) instruction for the country." A few years later a more definite precursor of the University Extension system appeared in the form of a pamphlet by the then Bishop of Bath and Wells, Lord Arthur Harvey, suggesting that the Mechanics' Institutes of the country, at that time flourishing bodies, should be supplied with lecturers from the Universities. The scheme however was premature.

The establishment of the system of Local Examinations, largely due to the suggestions of the late Sir Thomas Acland, created the first definite link between the Universities and the outside public; and the next step followed almost naturally. If the Universities agreed to examine their extra-mural students, could they not also give some definite system of teaching to them? And so the dawn of the organised University Extension system was at hand.

In 1867, Professor James Stuart, the "Father of

University Extension," as he is now almost universally called, began to evolve the whole modern system in response to an invitation received from the "North of England Council for promoting the Higher Education of Women," of which Mrs Josephine Butler and Miss A. J. Clough were respectively President and Secretary. The first connected courses of lectures were given by him at several towns in the north of England, and later in the same year were extended to working men at Crewe and Rochdale, the latter under the auspices of the "Rochdale Pioneers."

All the essential elements of the system were evolved during the course of these lectures by Professor Stuart's intuitive genius—the lecture, the class, the "paper work" and the syllabus. The scheme was placed in working form, no longer the "figment of a dream," before both the Universities and the towns of England, and their mutual co-operation was sought.

In 1872 the University of Cambridge took the definite step of appointing a Syndicate to consider the whole question and decided in favour of the adoption of the scheme. Four years later (1876) the University of London took a similar step, and in 1877 the University of Oxford took up the matter, though no very active progress was made for some years, 1885 marking the great development of its work.

And now, before tracing the further history and development of the movement, it will be desirable and essential to investigate its inner nature, to realise both its ideals and the means employed to realise them.

The avowed aims of the founders were, as has been

said, to bring the Universities to those members of the community who were unable to go to the Universities. It follows obviously that the effort must be imbued with the true University spirit, definiteness, earnest search after truth, careful weighing of evidence, real study; that the new development must be no mere series of popular lectures, highly valuable as these may be in their own place, but, on the other hand, should be an attempt to give thoughtful and expert, and, where possible, connected instruction of the University type, with a machinery which would exercise the personal energies of the students, so far as was compatible with the calls of their various avocations. And there was something more, and in this lies much of the extraordinary power which University Extension has exercised.

Just as in the Middle Ages, the thirst for knowledge arose, and scholars and eager youths thronged to the gradually forming centres, realising in most practical form the vital connection between "plain living and high thinking," so often disastrously ignored to-day, even so the ideal of Professor Stuart and his early co-adjutors and of all the succeeding workers has been, that a similar thirst for knowledge should be aroused, and to some extent satisfied, throughout the length and breadth of the country, and that life should thereby be enlarged and dignified and serve a new and higher purpose. That the individual should attain a higher and nobler development through the reasoned study of the great movements and thinkers of the past and present, and should at the same time receive a new equipment for his duties and responsibilities as a citizen, including a deep sense, through common intellectual interests, of the vital solidarity of the body politic.

These, and nothing less than these, were the ideals of the founders of University Extension, and at its highest, the work of the movement has both enshrined and developed them. Let us consider for a moment, how details of organisation have contributed to this.

In the first rank may be placed the voluntary character of the work. It may be necessary now to plead for State aid, but in the beginning the very effort required to start and maintain the lectures, quite unfettered except by University regulations, was a real strength in the towns. A few enthusiasts kindled a spirit of desire and the flame spread rapidly. It is a very doubtful point whether this could have occurred with a controlled and subsidised organisation, and it cannot be too much emphasised, that in any future developments voluntary work and co-operation must take the lead and be of first importance.

And then the unique character of the instruction must be studied, and this is especially necessary when we come to consider later the position at the present moment. The inspiration of the University Extension scheme is the triple plan of lecture, class and weekly paper work, finally consolidated by an examination with certificates awarded by the University to successful candidates.

This scheme, which at once stamps and differentiates University Extension from other agencies, provides obviously for instruction of the University type, for discussion of difficulties, and argument where needed, and for private study of the subject, revised in its outcome by the lecturer, and finally tested by examination papers set by an examiner other than the lecturer, the final award being made after consultation between them as to the character of the weekly paper work.

It is a most complete scheme. When carried out in its entirety, it forms a very satisfactory course of study; and it must be noted that only in rare instances are its advantages and force duly recognised by writers on the subject.

The usual plan adopted is rather to allude to University Extension as a more or less desultory type of instruction, of little intrinsic value, when in its real essence, it is the exact opposite.

We must pass on now, to survey briefly the history and development of the movement before dwelling in more detail upon its present position. Stated very generally, the development has proceeded on two lines, both of which form vital contributions. They may be termed the extensive and intensive factors, or in other words the stimulating and concentrating influences. To some extent it may be said that the University of Oxford has largely adopted the former method while Cambridge and London have pursued the latter. But no hard and fast line can be drawn, and one point cannot be too much emphasised, viz. that the University Extension work demands the intimate connection of both lines of progress.

The efforts of Cambridge and London have been

largely concerned with the maintenance of the minimum 12 lecture course and with consecutive and continuous grouping of such—also with the resultant grading of certificates, from the terminal to the Vice-Chancellor's, recognising three years of consecutive study, and culminating in the Affiliation certificate, which demands (1) the recognition of the town as an Affiliated Centre, (2) six terms work in one class of subject and two in another, and (3) additional examinations in two languages and elementary mathematics.

The privilege of three terms exemption from the ordinary University course and the remission of the Previous Examination is accorded to such affiliated students as desire to enter the University.

This affiliation scheme which was adopted enthusiastically by several centres, was the special creation of Cambridge. Oxford adopted it later, while London established a five year course of work and finally a Diploma in the Humanities.

The name of Dr R. D. Roberts of Cambridge will always be intimately associated with this development, into which he threw for years his incomparable energy and earnestness.

The University of Oxford was in the meantime proceeding along the other line of development. Under the inspiration of Sir M. Sadler and Mr J. A. R. Marriott, it was decided that, in order to foster the movement in small towns where the financial difficulty was great, the traditional 12 lecture course should be reduced to six.

This innovation met with immediate success; the Oxford work progressed by leaps and bounds; and it is still warmly advocated by the Oxford authorities, while at the same time they have endeavoured of late years to establish longer courses in addition.

The danger of this development lies obviously in the fact, that it causes the pendulum of study to swing over to the desultory side and so affords ground for the strictures passed by the critics of University Extension. On the other hand it is urged that stimulation and expansion are of vital importance.

The truth, as usual, probably lies between the extremes. Short courses are of the utmost value in certain cases, for arousing interest and meeting financial needs, but their establishment as a complete system would inevitably lower the standard, and nullify the educational aims of the movement, and also, in large measure, make it more difficult to secure financial aid from the State or Local Authorities.

An allusion must now be made to the part played by University Extension since its foundation in the establishment or development of other educational agencies. It unquestionably played a large part in the establishment of local University Colleges. The Firth College at Sheffield (1879) and the University College of Nottingham (1881) are direct results. The extension of the Yorkshire College at Leeds from a Science and Technical institution, into one including the humanities, was largely influenced by the University Extension work in the city; so that the present great University of Leeds may be considered in its origin as indebted to University Extension. Two flourishing local colleges, those of Reading and of Exeter, were in their

inception founded as definite University Extension institutions and with the latter must always be associated
the great work, both in founding and developing, of the
late Miss Jessie Douglas Montgomery. To these must
be added the Colchester College, now superseded by its
Technical successor.

Another most important movement of recent years,
the Workers' Educational Association, was very largely
derived from University Extension stimulation, while
the great development of Tutorial Classes directly
springs from the same source on its most intensive side.

We cannot forget either the employment of the
University Extension Lectures in many of the older
Settlements—Toynbee Hall being a striking example.
These instances bear emphatic testimony to the in-
herent vitality of the University Extension ideals; for
life must ever communicate life.

A further example of this quality is the development
of the system in our great sister world of the U.S.A.
It differs somewhat in organisation, but the differences are not essential, and the success is great. And
back from America came the conception, largely from
the Chautauqua annual assembly, of our Summer
Meetings. The idea was first developed by Oxford in
1888 and Cambridge followed suit.

The value of these meetings, in bringing together
students throughout Britain and from foreign countries,
into intimate relationships with one another and with
their respective problems, and their assemblage under
the instruction and influence of the best expert lecturers
and speakers cannot be estimated too highly; and the

development well combines those two sides of University Extension, the importance of which has been emphasised, the stimulating and the intensive.

We now pass to the last and all-important section of our subject, the present position of University Extension and its future possibilities.

In endeavouring to estimate these facts, the effect of the great European war cannot be ignored. It was a sternly testing time for every institution in the country, and none has emerged unaffected for good or evil.

With regard to University Extension complete destruction was prophesied by the pessimists. Lecturers would be called up, audiences would be engrossed in war work, finance would fail. But there were many, both at the headquarters in the Universities and in the centres, who took a different tone. A really necessary good thing cannot, because of its nature, fail. It may pass through storms of difficulty and be beaten to its very knees, but always "Truth is great and will prevail." And so it has proved.

The trial was great, the dangers immense, and both are still with us; but renewed life, and we believe a wider life has begun to appear, and our successors in the work, if not ourselves, will surely experience it. It must never be forgotten that the gallant attempt to "carry on" through the war was a great benefit to the community. The lectures had a calming and strengthening effect, as numerous testimonies witness, and in many centres the courses on history (especially of the belligerent nations, and of topics bearing on reconstruction problems) proved of most practical value.

We must now pass on to an as exhaustive and candid survey as possible, of the present situation. We ask what it exactly is? how far have old ideals been maintained? what are our present sources both of weakness and strength? what new developments are needed?

In analysing the present position it may be well first to consider the question not infrequently asked, "Is there room for University Extension among the numerous other Adult Education agencies, or is its day over?" The answer to this has been already given in outline, but a more detailed discussion may be of value. Any competition with Working Men's Colleges may be ruled out at once; the work done is of a different character.

We may say also that the Co-operative Educational activities—where they do not actually employ the University Extension agency—and the work of the Y.M.C.A. may be again placed in a non-competitive position.

There remains the work of the Tutorial Classes, the Lectures organised by the Gilchrist Educational Trust and some other bodies, and Settlement work. Between all these and the University Extension system there exist fundamental differences.

The *Tutorial Class* work, the original three years classes or the new "one year," are, in their very nature, more limited than University Extension desires to be. They are limited both as to numbers, and also more or less, as to the character of the classes which benefit by them. And the course of study is definitely intensive, and touches only one side of the University Extension work, which is directed to mixed audiences as large as possible, and reserves its intensive work for the class and writers of papers.

The courses of lectures organised by the *Gilchrist Trust* are avowedly "popular" and have no element of continuous study. Those arranged by *Settlements* are in some cases actually employing University Extension means, and in others are of a shorter and more fragmentary nature. The only serious rivalry to consider is in the matter of the "clientèle," but difficulties might also arise with regard to overlapping both in organisation and in finance. These difficulties could doubtless however be obviated, if sound systems of co-operation were established.

To be quite definite, the case of a town may be discussed where all the above agencies are active or willing to become so, University Extension Lectures, Tutorial Classes, Y.M.C.A. and an educational Settlement, with occasional lectures arranged by the Gilchrist Trust; also where plans are being made for carrying into effect the 1918 Education Act as regards day continuation classes for young persons between the ages of 16 and 18.

Now it is quite obvious, that in such a locality there would be considerable danger of overlapping, but also, that a well thought out scheme of co-operation might produce most excellent educational and social results.

If one might venture to suggest such a scheme, it would be of the following character, and could easily be adapted to localities where the circumstances slightly differed.

1. In the first place it would be necessary to form a central committee, consisting of representatives of the

various voluntary educational agencies and also of the Local Education Authority.

It would be the function of this committee to consider the needs of the town and then to draw up a scheme for any periods thought best, one year, three years, as might be, allotting to each agency its own special share.

2. The work of the Tutorial Classes and University Extension Lectures would be considered as mutually supplementary; the subject matter of each would be as far as possible in connection; the Tutorial Classes supplying in the main, though not entirely, the intensive side, the lectures the broader and more comprehensive aspect. "One year" classes and "short courses" of lectures might be added for stimulating purposes, as also occasional Gilchrist Lectures, if these could be granted. The members of the Tutorial Classes would by this means gain a variety in method and a desirable breadth of outlook, while the keener and more earnest of the University Extension students would be able to carry their studies forward in a definite direction.

By this means, not only would true co-operation be secured, but also a fusion of interests and individuals, which is much to be desired and absolutely within the scope and ideals of the two bodies.

More definite connection with the Universities should also be secured by this co-operation, and students both from Tutorial Classes and University Extension Lectures should be enabled, by the connected and continuous system of work, to take advantage of the Vice-Chancellor's or Affiliation Certificates, or any future means which may be devised, to take up residence in the Universities for one, two or three years, as the case might be. Any lecture schemes planned by the Y.M.C.A. or Educational Settlement could be arranged in accordance with the main scheme.

It cannot however be too strongly urged that each organisation should in such a scheme fully maintain its individuality and freedom. It is wise voluntary co-operation, not fusion, which is the desired aim.

It remains to speak of the help such a scheme would afford towards the effective carrying out of the Education Act in respect of continuation schools. Here would arise the opportunity of introducing strongly non-vocational study. It is surely absolutely essential, if the real objects of the Act are to be attained, that this should be done, for it would be disastrous beyond words, if the whole of the instruction in continuation schools should be on "vocational" lines. The wider aspects must be secured.

And in many ways the difficulty of an adequate supply of teachers would be lessened, if the services of University Extension Lecturers and Tutorial Class leaders could be employed. This would be in full accord with the recommendation of the Education Act, that in preparing schemes, "the local Education Authority shall have regard to the desirability of including therein arrangements for co-operation with Universities in the provision of lectures and classes for scholars, for whom instruction by such means is suitable."

It is in connection with this side of the question, as also with the financial one, that the presence of representatives of the Local Education Authority upon the central committees would be all important.

It is impossible within limited space, even were it desirable, to enter in any detail upon this essential subject of finance. But it may be urged that such a scheme of co-operation, as has been suggested, would go far towards the solution of the problem, both by tending to avoid the waste caused by competition and over-lapping, and also by making it possible to secure some well co-ordinated system of financial grants in aid, both from the State and the Local Authority.

It may be also contended that the function of University Extension would be a very special and important one in such a town scheme. For it already appeals to all sections of the community and includes them within its scope, so fulfilling the ideals animating all the modern views of Adult Education.

The so-called "leisured classes" need thought and knowledge intensely, if they are to overcome old prejudices and take a worthy part in the new national life. The "workers" demand the same; they cannot safely or adequately face their new and increasing re-sponsibilities otherwise. Our great army of teachers, both primary and secondary, require a strong and bracing atmosphere outside that of their own special vocation.

To our boys and girls on the verge of maturity it is of the highest importance that they should be stimulated by an influence to which they can yield themselves more fully in after-school life. And University Extension is well qualified to meet these varied needs, and to act both as a great combiner, and also as an inspiration to union and sympathy, those two crying needs of the present day.

We must now turn for a short time to the important, if possibly somewhat dull, subject of statistics, and endeavour to judge from the latest published Reports (1918–19) of the Universities on their Extension work, exactly how the movement stands. The Reports of Oxford, Cambridge and London will alone be considered, for the reason that the newer Universities, although in past years taking an important share in Extension work, seem now to be rather directing their energies, with respect to their extra-mural activities, towards Tutorial and one year Classes. During the Session 1918–19, we note that 121 Centres were in active work; 50 connected with Oxford, 36 with Cambridge and 35 with London. The number of courses of lectures was 60 in Oxford centres, 42 in those deriving from Cambridge and 103 in those associated with London—a total of 205.

The number of Lectures in these Courses varied considerably.

The *Oxford courses* consisted as a rule of six lectures, though a few extended to 10 or 12. These six lecture courses were very often linked together, so forming courses of twelve lectures occupying a whole session.

The large majority of the *Cambridge courses* contained 12 lectures. In the case of the three affiliated centres this number was enlarged to 24, and a small number of six lecture courses were also given.

The *London* returns note definitely 49 sessional courses of 24 or 25 lectures, 24 terminal courses of 10 or 12 lectures, and 30 of 5 to 7 lectures. The aggregate average attendances are given as *Oxford*, 8739, *Cambridge* 6149 and *London* 7818, a total of 22,706.

The number of certificates awarded was:

Oxford 21, and 89 "lists" given for six lecture courses.

Cambridge, 72 terminal, 3 Affiliation.

London, 364 terminal, 131 sessional and 12 diploma.

It must be noted in explanation of these last figures that no certificates are given for less than 10–12 lectures in a course, but that the Oxford Delegacy awards an inferior recognition, "Lists," for six lecture courses: also that the Affiliation certificates granted by Cambridge and the diploma of London are on much the same lines, demanding four sessions' lectures, including paper work and examinations in a final examination. The latter takes the form in the case of the London Extension Board of a survey of the work of the four sessions and in that of the Cambridge Syndicate of an examination in languages and elementary mathematics.

The place of the Affiliation certificate and the diploma is occupied in the Oxford scheme by the Vice-Chancellor's certificate which is on practically the same lines as the Affiliation certificate of Cambridge.

We pass now from statistics, which prove a very considerable amount of valuable work, to an enquiry into the general character and composition of the audiences. The numbers vary considerably, ranging from forty or fifty in small and struggling centres to 300 or

400 or more. The usual average may be taken as 80 to
200. As a rule the audiences are of a mixed character,
representing the different sections of the population, the
leisured classes, artisans, teachers, and the upper forms
of secondary schools. On the whole, women may be
said to predominate.

But there are a considerable number of centres where
artisans form the greater part, and in one or two cases,
such as Crewe, the whole of the audiences. Examples
of such are, Hetton-le-Hole, Fencehouses, Barnstaple,
Bideford, Northampton, Leicester, Bournemouth
(Winton), Chesterfield, Mold, Crewe, Swindon, Burslem, Longton, Stoke-on-Trent. Some of the statistics
for 1918–19 show large audiences in several of these
centres, and although it is not possible to state exactly
the proportion of artisans, still they very largely predominate. Examples of average audiences are: Hetton-
le-Hole, 440; Bournemouth (Winton), 100; Crewe,
250; Swindon, 140; Burslem, 152; Longton, 224. This
seems to betoken a desire that the intensive methods of
the Tutorial and one year classes should be supplemented in a more general direction. It is a further
proof of the contention raised previously, that there is
ample room for all the agencies of Adult Education.
The varied character of the audiences may be said to be
in exact accord with the ideals of the movement, which
aim at reaching all classes of the community.

We must now face the vital question of how far the
above statistics are satisfactory. Of course, it is obvious
that they are only so to a very limited extent. But it
must be remembered they represent conditions barely

emerging from the shadow of the great war, and also that there are, at the present moment, definite signs of a very marked advance in number both of centres and audiences and general renewed educational activity. One or two audiences rose in the Lent Term of 1919 to over 400 and have recently been surpassed. And yet the University Extension movement cannot be said to be fulfilling the ideals and hopes of its founders, of its leaders in the University departments, and of the devoted band of local organisers, while it is still so far from being co-extensive with the country, and even more, while its definite student work is so inadequate.

For the most cursory examination of the foregoing statistics reveals grave short-comings. 121 Centres, 205 Courses of lectures, attendances numbering 22,706 do not represent the activity necessary, if this form of adult education is to exert its possible influence. Still less do the number of certificates granted satisfy those who crave for real educational work.

These may be hard sayings; they may even be resented by the more flourishing centres, but this survey is of the work as a whole, and is written under an earnest desire to face the facts, surely the first step in any scheme of progress.

The first question to ask in this relation, is, what are the causes of these conditions and can they be transformed?

It is not an easy question to answer, for the causes are various.

1. Perhaps in the forefront may be placed the after-war conditions which include two opposite and yet

connected attitudes, apathy and weariness on the one hand and excitement and restlessness on the other. Neither are favourable to the desire for knowledge and steady thoughtful work, and yet both are only what might have been anticipated from the terrible years from which we have just emerged.

From many points of view, especially from that of the reasonable optimist, who is of untold value at the present time, these conditions may be regarded as transitory and in fact there are many signs that this is the case. Still they must be taken into account, and they call loudly for new educational enthusiasts, who throughout the towns and villages of the country will band themselves together as new University Extension pioneers, and feel as their predecessors did, that here is "a great school of service."

2. The second cause is unquestionably connected with Finance.

It has been proved over and over again a practical impossibility to maintain consecutive work of sufficient extent to satisfy real educational standards, without very large audiences. The fees required by the University authorities and which must be considerably increased if the most able lecturers are to be secured, together with continually increasing local expenses, form a heavy tax on the resources of ordinary centres, which in many cases ends or limits their activity. The almost natural result is a catering for popularity—short courses succeeding one another with startling variety—and the desire to secure lecturers with popular gifts. These expedients do not conduce to a high educational standard, and they do not draw in the most intellectual and true students. They are also, in large measure, responsible for the stigma sometimes cast, though most undeservedly, upon University Extension, that it is largely a mere system of popular lectures.

What is the remedy? To a certain extent local effort can do much by co-operation with other agencies—by earnest efforts to reach all sections of the population. Also a better organised grouping of centres will tend to eliminate the waste caused by excessive travelling on the part of the lecturers; equally bad for them and for the centres. This involves a certain sinking of individual preferences, and at times the risk of lectures, which, while desirable in one town, are not so in another.

The system of local University Extension Societies with regular subscribers is another excellent expedient. But more is necessary. Some regular system of aid from the State and from Local Authorities is urgently needed, and, if complete recognition is to be given to the movement, should be secured on an adequate scale.

Up to the present time, a certain amount of such help has been afforded, but by no means to a sufficient extent.

The Board of Education offers small subsidies, but the conditions are difficult to meet, and the amount offered hardly makes their fulfilment worth the labour involved. The grants made by the Gilchrist Trustees have similar drawbacks. A large number of Local Authorities, both County and Borough, also assist by small grants, or by providing lecture halls free of cost. In a few cases, e.g. Plymouth, Bournemouth, and one or two of the Potteries centres, the whole cost is defrayed by the Local Authority and all arrangements are in its hands.

In other cases, *e.g.* Portsmouth, the Local Authority guarantees the whole or part of any deficit. These are all steps in the right direction, but they are only partial and do not fully meet the need.

The Devon County Council has recently set apart £100 per annum for the assistance of needy centres—the grants to be both "block" and "capitation." A similar scheme is that of the Leicestershire County Council which offers a grant of £5 for each six lecture course and £10 for twelve lectures; and a capitation grant of 10s. and one of 20s. for each student attending respectively a course of six or twelve lectures and qualifying by class and paper work for the final examination, though not necessarily entering for it.

Now if this last scheme, or a similar one, could be adopted generally both by the State and by both Borough and County Education Authorities, if it could be on a generous scale, while coupled with inspection and also with representation on Local Committees, the financial difficulty and its attendant evils would be practically removed. There should be no diminution of voluntary zeal and energy, but the wearing strain would be relieved, the lectures could be planned in educational sequence, the student element would be increased by the stimulus of the variable grant, and a new life would be given to the movement.

It is of the utmost importance therefore, that in the new schemes of Local Authorities under the 1918

Education Act, the claims of the University Extension movement should be duly and adequately recognised, both in principle and by the system above suggested of adequate financial assistance.

The Act itself fully supports such a development, and such recognition. Another desirable development may be said to be the special function of the Universities. It concerns the status of the lecturers. A far greater measure of security is demanded if the best men are to be both secured and retained. Special qualities are needed for the University Extension lecturer, and many of these can only be gained by a long experience; but, under present conditions, a continued exercise of the work, with its very strenuous and often trying accompaniments, is difficult and demands often immense self-sacrifice.

No words can adequately convey what the University Extension movement owes to the strenuousness and devotion of its lecturers, but it is not fitting that such zeal should be over-strained and even exploited. Some system of a central fund, of fellowships, and of a distinct status, could surely be evolved to meet this urgent need; but so far only the most tentative steps have been taken towards it. Doubtless the difficulties are great; but the problem should not prove insoluble; and one thing is absolutely certain, that upon the capacity and high ability of the lecturers success or failure ultimately and fundamentally depend. And it is doubtful if this point is fully realised.

A summary of the developments needed, if University Extension is to take its necessary and fitting place in the adult education schemes of the future would accordingly include:

1. Adequate and co-ordinated financial assistance.

2. Full recognition and amendment of the present status of the lecturer.

3. Strengthened and adequate local organisation, united with a thorough co-ordination of all the educational agencies in the centre. University Extension should serve on the one hand the needs of all sections of the adult population, and on the other assist materially to meet those of the day continuation classes under the new Act.

4. Enthusiasm and effort to kindle and maintain the flame of the desire for knowledge in each town and village and to secure true educational efficiency.

These may be considered large demands, but the end is great and the means must be in proportion. And the end is worthy of effort. No local worker who has had a long experience of University Extension work doubts its power and importance for a moment. The actual testimony of the numbers who have come under its influence is unimpeachable.

"University Extension gave me a new view of life."

"I owe nearly all I have attained to the stimulus of the lectures."

"I owe to the University Extension movement more than I can ever express or repay."

Expressions such as these, and in large numbers, have been constantly received by local secretaries and workers of long standing, and they speak for themselves.

University Extension has great ideals, great prac-

tical possibilities, enormous capabilities. Its weak-
nesses are such as can be removed by thought and
effort. Its claims are unique in any national scheme of
adult education to meet the demands of all classes.
And experience has shown that it can, to use Mazzini's
fine words, "spur men to translate thought into action."

# IX

# THE TUTORIAL CLASS MOVEMENT

By W. G. CONSTABLE

Tutorial Class Tutor

A HISTORY and description of the Tutorial Class movement, like that of any other movement in education, can
give but a faint reflection of its real interest and
significance. Concerned as it must be largely with the
dry bones of organisation and method, it can only
occasionally reveal the energy and enthusiasm which
make those bones live and are the true cause of the
importance of the movement. It is not, indeed, my
purpose to discuss here the administrative and financial
problems connected with Tutorial Classes, nor to consider the place of the classes in the national educational
system. These matters are fully discussed elsewhere,
and I shall only refer to them so far as they bear upon
my object of explaining what a Tutorial Class is, and
the spirit that animates it; of giving some account of its
work; and of estimating critically its value as an educational and social institution.

As a starting point, a Tutorial Class may be described
as a class of working men and women who undertake
to study some subject on academic lines for a definite
period, under the guidance of a tutor appointed by a
University; and who further undertake to attend regularly and to do a certain fixed quantity of written work.

But before this definition can be understood, it is necessary to know something of the origin and development of the Tutorial Class movement.

The idea of extra-mural teaching organised by a University for students who are not members thereof, was first given its practical and systematic application in the University Extension movement, under the guidance and inspiration of Professor James Stuart, of Cambridge. The first intention of these classes was that they should primarily be for workpeople, and should possess some of the most important features of the Tutorial Class of to-day, viz. that the course should be continuous; that the lecture should be followed or preceded by a class; and that students should be required to do paper work. In practice these ideas were considerably modified; but, in the form it eventually took, the movement has achieved remarkable success, and shows no sign of diminishing in vigour and importance. For various reasons, however, though a considerable number of working men and women have been enthusiastic students, as a whole the working classes have been left untouched. In the first place, University Extension represents a side of University activity which attracts working people less than others do. On the one hand, a University is a centre of teaching, of the authoritative communication of knowledge already accumulated; on the other, it is a body of students united by the common aim of pushing back the frontiers of the unknown, and finding the means to a fuller and wider life—a society whose members feel themselves jointly dedicated to these aims and heirs to a great tradition. In practice, these two aspects are indissolubly connected; but in the University Extension movement the didactic side of University work has been more emphasised. This presupposes a certain level of education among the students and willingness to make certain fundamental assumptions; a course not justified with most working class audiences, who do not possess the educational apparatus needed to absorb University teaching in its ordinary form, and who approach that teaching in a distrustful and critical spirit. Moreover, the subjects of Extension lectures often seem to working people unimportant and unrelated to life as they know it. For these reasons, University Extension short courses are particularly unsuitable for working people; and the fact of little provision being made for class work means that there are few opportunities to deal with individual student's difficulties and to satisfy their critical spirit by question and answer. As the University Extension movement has been self-supporting, the class fees have had to be fixed at a higher figure than most working people could pay; and if a course is so popular as to attract an audience large enough for the fee to be comparatively low, it is *ipso facto* probably unsuitable for the working class. Consequently, there was room for an adaptation and development of University Extension, so that working people could profit from such teaching. The essential conditions were to emphasise the idea of union in pursuit of knowledge, in order to create confidence and avoid making unwarranted assumptions; to take the actual knowledge and experience of students as a starting point, and so bring teaching into close relation with their life; and to make instruction as continuous, systematic and individual as possible. Education on these lines the Tutorial Class seeks to provide. But it must be emphasised that there is no opposition between University Extension and Tutorial Class work. In their conception, in the ideas from which they spring, they are alike; and they are complementary parts of extra-mural University work. Their differences are dictated by practical considerations, and lie in machinery and method rather than in aim and spirit.

At the beginning of the century, it became tolerably clear that University Extension did not adequately meet working class needs. Meanwhile, working class demands for higher education had increased, a movement reflected in the formation in 1903 of the Workers' Educational Association; which is a federation of educational and working class organisations, and of individuals, designed to stimulate popular demands for education, and to organise the supply. It was mainly at the instance of this body, assisted by University men, that a committee was formed in 1907 consisting of members of the University of Oxford and of persons nominated by the Workers' Educational Association, to report on the relation of the University to the higher education of work-people. This committee reported in 1908, and with its report, the Tutorial Class movement may be said to have become a movement in being. Tutorial Classes were already in existence, however. In August, 1907, a class formed by the Rochdale branch of the Workers' Educational Association applied to

Oxford for a tutor. The members pledged themselves to study for three years, to attend twenty-four classes of two hours each during the year, and to write fortnightly essays. A tutor was appointed, and so the first Tutorial Class came into existence[1]. A little later, a class on similar lines was started at Longton. But the Oxford report really gave the movement coherence and definite shape. It laid down principles which have formed the basis of subsequent development; and the Joint Committee, which produced it, provided a means for the control and administration of Tutorial Classes, which has been taken as a pattern by other Universities. Since the publication of the report, the two classes of 1907–8 containing 78 students developed by 1914–15 into 155 classes with 3110 students. During the war, decline was inevitable; but a complete recovery has taken place, and in 1918–19, 153 classes were at work, embracing 3300 students. These figures are for the British Isles alone. In 1912, the movement gained a footing overseas, and in 1918–19 there were 54 classes established in Australia, 29 in New Zealand, one in Canada and two in South Africa. All did not conform exactly to the true Tutorial Class type: but all were conducted on similar principles. These figures alone, however, do not give an adequate idea of the growth of the movement. Many Tutorial Classes have given birth to subsidiary classes, similar in many respects to Tutorial Classes, conducted by Tutorial Class students. In Staffordshire, for

[1] It is interesting to notice that Rochdale was also the birthplace of another working-class movement of great importance, that of Consumers' Co-operation.

example, in 1918–19 there were 23 classes at work, containing 510 students, all of which owned the Longton class as parent. Elsewhere, after officially coming to an end, Tutorial Classes have been carried on in an informal way as a kind of Study circle.

It has been seen that the first Tutorial Classes were established under the University of Oxford. By 1913–14, all Universities in England and Wales, the Queen's University, Belfast, and several University Colleges were conducting classes. Since that date, the Universities of Edinburgh and Aberdeen have joined in the movement. Oxford, London, Leeds, Liverpool and Manchester have the largest number of classes. As would be expected, the movement is most vigorous in the industrial districts of the North and Midlands. Here, with men and women thrown into close contact, and a higher level of material prosperity than elsewhere, there have developed a wider sphere of interests and greater incentives to acquire knowledge; and it has been easier to organise classes and for students to attend them. Tutorial Classes have, indeed, been successful in country areas; but there the initial obstacles to organisation and the physical difficulties of carrying on the class have prevented the movement making the same headway. Broadly speaking, all Universities save Oxford and Cambridge serve the districts from which they draw most of their intra-mural students. Oxford and Cambridge have established classes in widely separated districts not served by other Universities.

Turning now to consider the organisation of a Tutorial Class, a basic principle of the movement up to the present has been that a class should only come into existence in answer to a spontaneous demand. This demand has generally come through the Workers' Educational Association, but occasionally from some other working class body or from an Adult School; and the organisation which asks for the class is responsible for its formation and management. The importance of this principle is twofold. By throwing a large part of the responsibility for the inception and conduct of the class upon its members, it gives some guarantee of steady application and continuous effort; and, by emphasising the idea of joint effort on the part of tutor and students, establishes confidence that the class will obtain the kind of education it seeks.

A class is now definitely limited to thirty-two members and is generally formed for three years; though there is nothing to prevent a class going on for a longer period if circumstances warrant this being done. Twenty-four lectures are delivered each year during the winter months, at weekly intervals, and the members pledge themselves to attend regularly unless prevented by unavoidable causes such as overtime or illness; and they undertake to do an essay or some equivalent form of written work every fortnight. The meetings of the class are generally held in the evenings, after the day's work, and last for two hours, the first of which is devoted to a lecture, the second to a discussion carried on by the class as a whole. In these ways, the distinctive aims of a Tutorial Class can be secured, viz. continuity of study; the active co-operation of students in the work as distinct from mere passive attendance at a lecture;

and teaching which is individual and definitely tutorial in character.

The members of a class are all adults, may be either men or women, and mainly belong to the working classes. There are no general statistics available of the age of students, but particulars of individual classes suggest that most students are between twenty and forty, and of these again the majority are under thirty. In the British Isles, in 1913–14, of the 3234 students enrolled, 746 were women; in 1917–18, of 2860 students, 1179 were women. The rapid rise in the proportion of women is due, of course, to the war. In 1913–14, of 3035 students, 623 were clerks and telegraphists, 308 were teachers, 160 shop assistants, 193 women working at home, 1278 employed in some form of skilled manual labour. In 1917–18, of 2860 students, 414 were clerks and telegraphists, 438 teachers, 250 housewives or domestics, 70 shop assistants and 919 engaged in skilled manual labour. Here again, differences in composition are probably to some extent due to the war, and to the increased proportion of women students.

The tutor of the class is appointed by the Joint Committee of the University concerned. The composition of the Committee, and the fact that it has joint secretaries, one a University man and the other a working class representative, emphasises the co-operative principle in the conduct of the classes. The tutors are either regular members of the University staff who take one or two tutorial classes in addition to their ordinary work; men and women engaged in other occupations who take one or two classes; and University graduates who devote practically their whole time to the work. The type of tutor varies somewhat with the University. Oxford for instance mainly appoints full time tutors, while none of the Cambridge tutors are of this kind. The level of qualifications required also varies. Some Universities insist on the tutor being qualified to take intra-mural work; others are not so critical.

The subjects studied by Tutorial Classes cover a wide range. In 1918-19, out of 153 classes, 54 were studying Economics or Industrial and Social History; 20 Psychology and Philosophy, 27 English Literature, and 15 Modern European History. Other subjects taken were Biology, Political Science, Music, and Problems of Reconstruction. The first notable thing about these subjects is that they are primarily political and social in character. It is natural that this should be so. The demand for adult education by working people has largely been inspired by a desire to understand and explain the meaning of what goes on in everyday life around them—a desire stimulated by increased political power and growing consciousness of its possession; and in every walk of life, the tendency is for the seeker after knowledge to base his quest upon what he is most familiar with and considers most important. Moreover, such subjects as economics and history do not, like classics or mathematics, call for a long and wearisome acquisition of a technical apparatus. A second important characteristic of the subjects is that they are non-technical and non-vocational. Their study does nothing directly to increase a student's earning power, or to enable him in the narrow sense of the term "to better" himself socially or financially. This marks a difference between the Tutorial Class and the Technical or Evening School. As a whole, the Tutorial Class movement represents a demand for education for its own sake; for satisfaction of that hunger for knowledge which is caused by a desire to solve the problems of existence, to make life fuller and richer, and to cultivate habits of mind which make towards a wiser conduct of life. It is true that some students come to a Tutorial Class with narrower ends in view. For example, the considerable number of students engaged in some form of public voluntary work such as Trade Unionism, Co-operation, or Local Government, sometimes join a class merely to acquire knowledge which will be directly useful in this work. But in most cases this intention develops into a genuine enthusiasm for education apart from its immediate value; and in any case the original motive for coming to the class was not one of selfish material advantage.

Coming now to the actual method of conducting a Tutorial Class, though in theory somewhat hard and fast lines are laid down, in practice there is considerable elasticity. The four elements in Tutorial Class work are the lecture or formal instruction; the discussion in which students bring forward their own views, ask questions on the subject of the lecture, or seek for information on allied matters; the essay, written by the students in their own time, based in part on the lectures but mainly upon their own experience and reading; and individual tuition. These four elements are mingled by the tutor in the way he considers best suited to the needs and circumstances of the class. In this respect, everything depends upon the constitution of the class. For example, when it is tolerably homogeneous in character and ability, and the members are not unduly diffident, more formal methods may be adopted with advantage than when there are wide differences in age, ability and temperament. In this case, the tutor must adopt such a course as will best ensure each student profiting to the greatest extent from the teaching. Usually Tutorial Classes, unlike classes in a University, contain widely different kinds of mind and experience; so that informal and elastic methods have to be the rule.

The work of the class is generally based on a syllabus prepared by the tutor, which may be elaborate and detailed or a simple collection of headings. My own experience is that a detailed syllabus does not in fact hinder necessary adaptations and variations; and has the advantage of giving students a coherent and reasoned outline of the ground they are to cover, which is particularly useful when there is no satisfactory text-book available. It also allows the tutor to assume a knowledge of the general structure of his argument, and frees his hands to develop the more difficult or interesting parts of a subject. The lecture itself may be formal and continuous, or broken by questions from the tutor or from the class. A lecture read or delivered from detailed notes is rarely successful. It must be remembered that nearly all the students have a long and tiring day's work behind them, and that every effort must be made to keep their attention and interest. This is an argument

in favour of encouraging questions when a point is not
clear, or of the tutor asking the class for suggestions or
illustrative examples.  Another point to keep in mind
is that Tutorial Class work assumes independent study
on the part of the student.  The lecture, therefore, need
not aim so much at conveying information, as at stimulating interest, and providing guidance and encouragement to the student's own work.  The fault of trying to
put too much into a lecture is particularly to be avoided
in Tutorial Class work.  Another factor which influences
the form of the lecture is that the class is not studying
for an examination as is generally the case with University
students; so that the tutor can afford to concentrate on
matters of special importance or of particular interest to
the class.  For example, in studying history, a better
grip of the subject may be gained by the intensive study
of one or two periods, with some reference to original
authorities and with special attention to method, than
by a hurried and necessarily superficial survey of a longer
period.  The students, armed with the material provided
by such study, may be left to fill the gaps by their own
reading, their knowledge being tested by written work.

In maintaining and stimulating the interest of the
class, however, the tutor must not forget that the
lecture is primarily intended for the instruction of the
class as a whole, and that he must then, more than at any
other time, maintain his position as leader of the class.
For example, he must not allow himself to be side-
tracked into dealing at too great length with small
points or with individual difficulties.  In other words,
a sense of proportion must be steadily maintained.  In

the discussion which follows and is based upon the lecture, more freedom is allowable and desirable. But here again the tutor must keep control and direction. The tendency is frequently for one or two students of marked ability or force of character to monopolise the talk, in order to satisfy their own thirst for knowledge, to acquire information for some particular purpose, or sometimes, to expound their own particular political and social views. Consequently, the tutor by inviting other students to contribute or by timely questions, should keep the discussion as general and as much to the point as possible, to enable everyone to benefit therefrom. But however well the discussion may be directed, it cannot supply the place of individual tuition. Unfortunately, this is always very difficult to arrange in Tutorial Classes. The members are very rarely free except on Sundays and in the evenings, and the tutor is generally only in the town or village where the class is held for a short time. My own practice has been to meet students both before and after the class; and the hospitality which was freely given me also gave opportunities for giving help and advice to individuals. It cannot be emphasised too strongly how essential it is for a Tutorial Class tutor to know individually each member of his class. By knowing the character and attainments of each student, not only can he help the diffident and retiring to develop into vigorous members of the class, but he can direct energy and enthusiasm, which sometimes threaten to be hindrances, into useful and productive channels.

The fortnightly essay also affords a useful peg on which to hang individual tuition. It is a truism to say that in education teaching is unimportant as compared with learning; and by the essay the real value to the students of the lecture and class is tested, and the extent to which they have read and thought about a subject for themselves. The subjects of Tutorial Class essays are generally chosen, not so much to prove a knowledge of actual facts as to ensure that knowledge gained has been thoroughly assimilated, to encourage original thought, and to train students in bringing a critical and dispassionate mind to bear upon a subject. To secure these aims, considerable elasticity in handling is desirable. It is often better for a student to write three or four long and careful essays during a session, embodying perhaps some original research, than the full number of shorter ones; while those whose primary need is practice in expression benefit most by frequent writing of short essays on easy subjects.

Apart from considerations of this kind, external circumstances such as overtime may make regular written work almost impossible; in which case, the writing of essays as opportunity offers must be accepted. But however elastic the actual system adopted may be, there is no doubt that written work must be insisted upon. Without it, the student tends to become a mere passive recipient of odds and ends of information. He is never forced to think over or to organise what he has read or heard, and so gets little or no benefit from it. The tutor must therefore be prepared to give as much help as possible in the essay work, and especially set himself to overcome the *vis inertiae* arising from defective elementary education.

From the essays the standard of work in Tutorial Classes may best be judged. In object and method, the classes are similar to those held inside a University. They aim not merely at imparting knowledge, but at training and developing the student's mind and judgment; and for this purpose, the teaching should be impartial and detached in character, undertaken in a spirit of high seriousness, and based on critical examination of fundamental facts. But how far the work of Tutorial Classes is comparable to that produced in a University, it is difficult to say. Allowance must be made for the fact that the majority of students lack the literary foundation possessed by University students; though they bring to their work a more extensive knowledge of the realities of life. Also, while the University man is generally reading for an examination or to fit himself for some profession, the Tutorial Class student has other ends in view. Add to this that the obstacles to private study are often serious. It is not easy after a long day's work, to absorb a difficult book or to write an essay; and when, as is generally the case in working class houses, there is only one sitting-room, shared by all the family, the difficulty is increased. In the case of married men and women, family duties are bound to occupy much of their spare time. Some of the students in my own classes generally waited until the rest of the family had gone to bed, before being able to begin work. Another difficulty is the supply of books. A few text-books the student may buy; but large books and original authorities are beyond his means. To keep a class of thirty-two people supplied is, however, more than

Universities and Local Authorities have so far been able
to do.

It follows that definite comparison of Tutorial Class
essays with (say) those written by the average candidate
for honours in a University is almost meaningless. The
only test applicable is the general impression of those
most competent to judge—such as the tutors, and
inspectors of the classes. On the whole it can be said
that Tutorial Classes come out of the comparison
favourably. This was the opinion of Mr Headlam and
Professor Hobhouse, who inspected the classes for the
Board of Education in 1913[1]; and is likewise the view
expressed in the report of the Adult Education Committee, 1919[2]. On the other hand, while much really
good work is being done in Tutorial Classes, there is
also a great deal of work which is very inferior. Tutorial
Class students are merely men and women; and it is
doing the movement no service whatever unduly to
exaggerate its achievements, as there is a tendency to do
in certain quarters. It is more important to couple with
an understanding of the movement a critical examination of its methods and results, in order to ensure that
development takes place in the best direction.

In such an examination the fundamental characteristics of the classes must be remembered. They are
composed of men and women already earning their own
living, who for the most part want knowledge for its
own sake and for the explanation it gives of the facts of
life as they know them; and who are critical, probably
biased, and possibly hostile to the tutor. Consequently,

[1] Quoted in *Report*, § 116.      [2] *Report*, §§ 107—116.

the note of co-operation must always be struck in the conduct of the class. The tutor must avoid a pontifical attitude, or the undue use of authority as the justification for assertions. The students should feel that they and the tutor are engaged in a joint quest, wherein the tutor by virtue of certain opportunities and capacities is the leader. I have already mentioned how the fact that a class comes into existence on the initiative of a working class organisation, and the composition of the Joint Committee, make a useful foundation for the development of this co-operative spirit. It can be fostered by such means as encouraging students to write papers embodying original research; by the secretary of the class being also a member thereof; by arrangements for the distribution of books being in the hands of the class; and by the encouragement of informal meetings of students to discuss essay subjects or topics arising out of the lectures.

Throughout his work, the tutor must be as impartial and fair-minded as possible, and in particular must avoid any suspicion of propaganda. But without being too dogmatic, he should have the courage of his convictions. Criticism must never be resented, but rather welcomed and met. Once a tutor feels that a Tutorial Class is accepting what he says without question or comment, he may be certain something is going wrong—the students are either neglecting what he says or discounting its value. So long as his lectures arouse vigorous and sustained discussion, all is well; and if as a result he can see some practical matter treated in a different spirit, he can be satisfied. Tact and patience are also indispensable qualities in a tutor. His class is often tired and apt to be querulous, and some of its members have strong prejudices based on bitter experience. But often the most difficult student in the end becomes the best ally and most trustworthy supporter, by reason of the very qualities which made him a hostile critic. The tutor must always be a master of his subject, well up to the level of intra-mural teachers. In the subjects studied by many Tutorial Classes, the students' knowledge of some branch is often very considerable; and unless the tutor can meet them on an equal footing, he will never keep his leadership. At the same time, he should not hesitate to admit ignorance, doubt or error; and always be ready to fill gaps in his knowledge, or to answer questions, by special research. Only in this way can he gain the real confidence of his class.

The question of the relation of the tutor to the University is a more difficult one to settle. The different types of tutors I have already described. In my own opinion, the tutor should be closely in touch with work inside the University. There are strong arguments in favour of whole-time tutors living in the district where the classes are held; especially because they are able to organise individual tuition more satisfactorily. But the great danger is that these men should become a class apart, living, so to speak, on the fringes of the University, but having no real part nor lot in its life. They tend to become regarded as on the whole inferior to intra-mural teachers; and since their opportunities for contact with the best minds of the day and for research are necessarily limited, this tendency is to some extent justified. Thus if

Tutorial Classes were entirely or mainly in the hands of whole-time tutors, instead of being treated as an integral part of the work of the University, they would become a water-tight compartment, and their vitality and energy, so far as they depend upon constant and real contact with the life and thought of a University, would be impaired. The tutor is the true and essential link between the University and the classes; and nothing should be done to hinder that function. Moreover, each side of a tutor's work—the intra-mural and the Tutorial Class work—benefits the other. Each is a means of preventing the other getting into a rut. Whether his work inside the University is teaching or research, the experience of external work will test its value; and the external work will benefit from being constantly stimulated by thought and study within the walls of the University.

Another danger which has arisen is, lest anxiety to increase the number of Tutorial Classes should cause tutors of inferior quality to be appointed. The argument that it is better to have a poor class than no class at all, emphatically does not apply to Tutorial Classes. A policy based thereon only weakens and discredits the whole movement. Consequently if the movement is to develop and retain its character, the Universities must be prepared to find suitable tutors, by increasing the number of members of their intra-mural staff, who take part in Tutorial Class work.

But though the future of the Tutorial Class movement depends very much upon the tutor, it no less rests in the hands of the students. They on their side must cultivate the spirit of humility which distinguishes the real seeker after knowledge, and must strive to be as open-minded and unprejudiced as possible. They must remember that in fact the Universities are the repositories of the University tradition, and that whatever their faults may be their guidance and authority must, to some extent, be taken on trust. In particular, any members of the class who seek to use it as a field for social or political propaganda, must learn to modify their attitude, if the movement is to achieve its real aims. The class must also be prepared to take really seriously the pledge they have given to attend regularly, and to work steadily in their spare time. Serious study is bound to have its arid patches, which must be traversed cheerfully without shirking; otherwise, students only acquire a smattering of knowledge, and leave the class thinking they know something of a subject, when they have barely touched its fringes. This not only discredits the movement as a whole, and frustrates its object, but is dangerous in spreading a false standard and conception of education.

So far, I have considered only the internal conditions upon which the success of a Tutorial Class depends. External conditions, such as the relation of the classes to the University and to the Board of Education, are equally important; but with them I do not propose to deal as they are considered in detail elsewhere. Some external conditions, however, so closely affect the internal work of a class, that they must be mentioned here. Though determination can overcome some of the difficulties in the way of private study, persistent overtime will always hinder regular attendance and systematic essay writing; and unemployment, or changes in the place of employment almost invariably mean serious breaks in a course of study. At present, however, factors such as these must be accepted as inevitable elements in Tutorial Class work, and arrangements made to meet them. In this connection the movement towards a general reduction in working hours is of great importance.

Reference has already been made to the problem of the supply of books. It is certain that students cannot themselves provide all the books required. At present, the University concerned sends a certain number of volumes, and on occasion Local Authorities have been helpful. But the supply is generally inadequate to meet the demand, and so the work of a class is often seriously hampered. The matter cannot be dealt with by individual classes or local organisations, partly because of expense, and partly because books purchased for one class could not easily be utilised at the end of the course. A central organisation, however, supplying a considerable number of classes, can almost invariably keep most of its books in circulation. Such organisations exist, both in the Universities and outside; but their value is limited by lack of funds[1]. The matter is really one that needs dealing with on a large scale, and in conjunction with other financial questions.

I have already mentioned the difficulties which arise in a class from lack of a tolerably uniform level of

[1] The Central Library for Students, Tavistock Square, W.C., is the most important.

education among Tutorial Class students. Not only do individuals fail to get the best from the class, but the class as a whole is injured by time and effort having to be spent in dealing with elementary difficulties. Nothing of any kind ought to be done to impair variety of outlook among members of a class, making, as it does, for vigour and enthusiasm: but that students should have some knowledge of how to read, and of how to express themselves orally and on paper, is most desirable. It is noticeable that in classes where the difference in ages is large, difference in other respects is also great. This suggests that as time goes on, and the influence of elementary education has had time to work itself out, the difficulty will tend to disappear. In this connection, the establishment of continuation schools should have valuable results, in providing a bridge between the elementary school and some form of adult education. Meanwhile, the establishment of some form of preparatory class for Tutorial Classes has much to recommend it. Experiments in this direction have been made already, and have proved their value. These classes should aim, not so much at imparting information, as at developing the confidence of students, and giving them practice in reading, digesting what they read, and expressing what they have to say. To make them a kind of elementary Tutorial Class would be a mistake; they should rather be definitely preparatory thereto.

Another important development of Tutorial Classes is the Summer Schools held by some Universities during the summer, and open to Tutorial Class students. Here, for a brief period they are able to devote the whole of their time and energies to study, amid surroundings entirely suitable for the purpose. A certain part of the course consists of lectures, in many cases delivered by specialists; the remainder of private tuition, and the discussion of essays or similar work written by the student. Thus, as far as possible, the conditions under which an internal student lives and works are reproduced. The benefit which members of a Tutorial Class derive from such a visit is considerable. They are brought directly into touch with the atmosphere of a University, and come to feel as never before, a sense of community with, and participation in, its aims and ideals. Apart from any specific knowledge they may gain, they carry away with them an understanding of what a University means, the memory of friendships and of contact with other minds, which stimulates and strengthens enthusiasm and gives courage to face and overcome difficulties. Whether the Tutorial Class will, in the future, serve as a channel for bringing work-people to a University as internal students, it is difficult to say. A few members of Tutorial Classes have proceeded to a University; but under present educational and economic conditions these cases must be regarded as exceptional. It is probable, however, that in the future the movement in this direction will become increasingly important.

Discussion in detail of the social effects and significance of the Tutorial Class movement is outside the scope of this essay, and would raise the whole question of the bearing of adult education upon national welfare. It is enough to point out that for good or evil, democracy in some form or other has come to stay, and that its future depends upon the development of wisdom and virtue among the people as a whole. Thus the problem of adult education is one of the most serious and pressing of the many problems which await solution to-day. Education has got to be regarded in a new light; not merely as a question of what and how children at school shall be taught, but as a force always at work helping to determine the conduct of men and women. Evidently the responsibility of the Universities is a heavy one. They cannot, even if they wish, stand outside of the main stream of national life. They must be prepared to descend into the arena, and put their resources at the service of the community as a whole. Not that the Universities should become centres of purely technical or vocational training; but while maintaining the great tradition of the value of knowledge for its own sake, their work should be definitely and clearly related to the activities of the world around them. The real question is whether the initiative is to come from the Universities themselves, or from those who, though doubtless moved by excellent intentions, yet have neither knowledge nor understanding of what a University stands for, and how it can best perform its functions. That the Tutorial Class movement solves the whole problem of the relation of the Universities to the working classes, is a wholly extravagant claim; but that it is one of the most fruitful educational experiments of recent years is certain.

Through the Tutorial Class not only are knowledge and character directly influenced, but a real concern for and interest in education are developed; and vague aspirations are clarified, defined, and tested, so that they become real and active forces in life. Also, by coming into direct contact with a University working people come to understand that Universities are not effete institutions maintained for the benefit and pleasure of the wealthy, but homes of a great tradition, and centres of devotion to ideals and of unsparing labour. Thus future extensions of University activities will find a growing body of opinion in the country which is likely to be informed and sympathetic. On the other hand, the University gains by contact with working people. They bring, into what is apt to be a somewhat rarefied and intellectually exclusive atmosphere, a certain sense of reality, a first hand familiarity with the hardest facts of life, which is refreshing. Moreover, if the Universities are to play that part in adult education which they ought to play, they must have a real understanding of working class conditions and needs. One of the channels through which this may come is the Tutorial Class. Armed with such knowledge and experience, the Universities can then face the future without fear, knowing that, if they perish, it will be for all that is best in them and not through their mistake or ignorance.

# X

# A STUDENT'S EXPERIENCE

## By ALFRED COBHAM

### A FOREWORD

This Essay is written from the point of view of a working-man, a craftsman with a lifelong experience of working-men of the wage-earning class.

I know the difficulties and soul-destroying conditions that surround the lives of very many of the workers; I know the oppression and languor of unvarying toil at uninteresting and unpleasant tasks, the jading weariness of repeating the same mechanical movements every minute for fourteen hours a day, month after month, year after year. I know what it is to see my boyhood and youth pass away without any opportunity for education such as the Forster Act gave to those of later birth. I know what it is *not to know*, and to be conscious of not knowing, what it is to feel a real mind-hunger. I have many times stood wistfully, cravingly looking into a book-shop window much as a penniless urchin looks into that of a confectioner. I have known these things and I sometimes ponder them regretfully. There is this consolation, however. The opportunity came to me when I understood the need for it, and I sometimes even feel thankful that I was not born in better circumstances. I might have had a "sound business education" thrust upon me and lost my soul; I was, in fact, lured into the verdant fields of literature where I found its appropriate sphere.

For twenty-five years I have lived in a University Extension atmosphere doing University Extension work, and it has brought into my life a great joy, which is ample justification for my plea for widespread Adult Education.

## ADULT EDUCATION

Of all questions in which the commonwealth is concerned, none has so completely and so suddenly passed from political obscurity into the full blaze of public discussion as adult education.

As if in amends for past centuries of neglect, this great question has now become so prominent, that it is the leading topic in newspaper articles and the speeches of political propagandists. A committee of the Ministry of Reconstruction has carefully considered and reported upon the question; and has published interim and final reports which should be read by all.

The question is one that especially concerns the workers who for centuries have been neglected, except for such tentative and philanthropic efforts as are indicated in the Report. But now the necessity of adult education is being loudly proclaimed from the platforms of every political creed, and in after-dinner speeches at civic functions.

It is not always true that in the multitude of councillors there is wisdom; it is certainly not true when councillors are eager to set up false aims and offer opposing schemes, tainted sometimes with the canker of narrow selfishness or class interest. When there is a lower and narrower ideal than that of national life, only the high hand of authority can balance between the contending parties; only a recognised power can include or reject any of the theories so zealously advocated.

This much, however, seems to have been established that education is the right of every individual; that the education of the individual is a benefit to the community; and that the means of education should be provided without reference to age for all those past the compulsory limit.

History has proved that ignorance is a menace to the government and a danger to the community. Ignorance it was that destroyed the newly invented machinery that was designed to supersede human labour. The ignorant have ever been foolishly conservative, suspicious of reform, or reckless in overturning institutions when the spirit of revolution prompted their action. Ignorance is too great an evil for a wise government to ignore. The Report, which is the occasion of these Essays, outlines a grand scheme of adult education. This may well prove to be the people's charter of intellectual life, the herald of a new and better day for the workers.

There must be no low-roofed ideals in this new empire of mind. Education must be as wide as the universe and as high as heaven; it must function for life towards the highest and noblest ends. It is of the utmost importance to understand the true nature of education in general, and also of the form in which it may be best administered to the working population in particular.

Low and deficient ideas of the whole subject have prevailed in the past, and are not yet wholly exploded.

There is just now a good deal of interest being taken in the question by that enterprising progeny of the industrial revolution, Incubus, Gradgrind and Co. They tell us that "if we are to hold our own in the markets of the world we must concentrate our efforts upon technical education." Works-schools and similar schemes are proposed built on the model of the pre-war German system. This "workshop of the world" cult would "standardise" the worker's mind as it has done his hand in the interests of trade.

The workers are rightly suspicious of suggestions of this kind, and are alert to the irony of the huckster's wiles. Now while I agree that we must cultivate the industrial and commercial side of our national life, and strive to excel in the markets of the world, let us never forget that the great aim of education should be not trade, but life. Trade is incidental, but a country is not made great by its tradesmen, but by its poets, artists, inventors and statesmen. By all means let us have vocational training and restore, if we can, something of the spirit and skill of the mediaeval craftsman, but, more than that, let us learn to understand and appreciate the higher values of life, and strive to realise the best.

By the term education it is not intended only to mean that men may become the better qualified to "speed up" production. Education stands for something greater than that. It is the drawing out, the discipline, and due development of all the faculties and affections of man's nature, so as to prepare him for the right discharge of

whatever attaches to his place in life. Technical education we must have, but let us not, in concentrating on
this side of our life, stunt the growth of the nobler
qualities. It has been the great mistake of the past that
the intellect has been cultivated, and the heart neglected,
as if the emotions were not as much a constituent of our
nature as the intellectual faculties. I once heard Prof.
Leonard say, "What the world needs so much to-day is
hard-headed hearts, and soft-hearted heads." If we are
to get the greatest enjoyment and the best practical
results from education, the heart must co-operate with
the head in producing a character in harmony with the
best teachings of history and the highest conception of
life, and to this end education must be wisely organised
and efficiently administered.

Much stress is being laid on citizenship as the aim
and end of education. Indeed the Report declares that
"citizenship must be the goal of all education." Like
the word "patriotism" at the beginning of the war, the
word "citizenship" looms large just now in the speeches
of politicians prospecting for national reconstruction.
As one hears the over-emphasised repetition of the word
in inaugural addresses at middle class union meetings,
one wonders for what it stands in the minds of these too
suddenly over-anxious "elevators of the people." There
can be no widespread ambition for citizenship where
there is not a high and noble ideal of citizenhood, and
there can be no worthy conception of citizenhood which
does not comprehend democratic culture, economic
justice, and social equality. We may instruct our adult
workers in civics, economics, sociology, industrial

history, and so forth. It is all very good and very necessary, but the urgent, imperative need of the hour is a civic conversion and the birth of a democratic soul. I know there are many of the workers who interpret these ideals with a class-conscious prejudice. They would prostitute education to ignoble ends. Out of the elements of knowledge they would fashion a weapon with which to wrest the golden calf from the idolaters that they themselves may fall down and worship it. With their materialistic conception of life and economic interpretation of history they would reverse all the holiest principles of religion and morality, and lower the standard of manhood to the level of the brute. There must be no vulgar ideals of citizenship in the reconstructed city. If the world is to be made safe for democracy, it must be the immediate purpose of education to make democracy safe for the world, and that can only be done by tuning the faculties of the mind to the emotions of the heart.

Nothing more disastrous has ever befallen this nation than the alienation of moral considerations from economic theory. The assumption that self-interest is the prime motive of human action has been a greater curse to England than all the ten plagues were to Egypt. Its results are seen alike in the East end and in the West. It has sullied the beauty of our country and poisoned the English soul, and its maxims may be read in the hard, sullen countenances of its votaries. "Buy in the cheapest market; sell in the dearest"; "Every man for himself and the devil take the hindmost." These, and such as these, make up the decalogue of the infamous code of "commercial morality." Self-sacrifice, not self-interest, must be the keynote of the reconstructed world. This is the example and the legacy of the dead heroes in Flanders. Their names cut deep in the granite memorials in the Town Hall squares of the cities and towns of England will ever give the lie direct to the economic heresies, which have been drummed and trumpeted into the unthinking heads of the people for a century and a quarter.

What we need to realise is that the individual is created to be something more than a "cog" in a wheel, or a "hand" in an industrial system, or even a citizen in a nation of shopkeepers. He is a human being with a soul and an imagination that have their needs apart from the demands of trade, or the requirements of the State. Man should be educated as man, and not merely as a mechanic or citizen, though these are factors in his manhood. There are within him great powers that transcend these. Citizenship is not enough. Besides, as the greater includes the less, it will be found that the mind which has been trained to the most complete views of life, to take in the wide scope of its being, will be ever the best fitted to fulfil the special duties of worker and citizen. We may instruct the workers in the wide range of technical science, and the niceties of mathematical calculation. We may teach them the history of the Aryan migrations, and the origin and growth of nations, of the social evolution of mankind from the cave-dweller to Karl Marx. We may inform them (cautiously) on the theory of rent, the critical margins of production and exchange, and the meaning of "spot"-prices on the market; but unless they are inspired by a desire to use this knowledge for the public weal and in the higher services of life, citizenship will never rise above the level of Drudgetown or Vanity Fair.

It must be the aim of education to teach men to interpret life in terms of life, that they may learn to love life and all its manifestations in air and earth. Teach man to gaze upon and wonder at the beautiful universe of which he is a part. The waltzing movements of the stars, the radiant splendour of the sun, the marvellous beauty of the flowers, the gorse-clad moorland, the clover-spangled meadows, the rippling river, and the mountain mist. Quicken his imagination, that the creature may become a creator, and he will go whistling to the plough, the anvil, the loom, with a glad heart and a willing hand and citizenship will realise itself. The soul of a poet is worth more than the combined intellect of a dozen politicians, even from the Gradgrind point of view. But, whether or not,

All parts away for the progress of souls: all religion, all solid things, arts, governments, all that was or is apparent upon this globe or any globe, fall into niches and corners before the procession of souls along the grand roads of the universe.

It may be said that all this is "in the clouds." The practical politician will demand "facts" and "practical" schemes. Henceforth I shall be intensely practical. To begin with, let me say that I endorse the Report. I think it is one of the most promising documents that has issued from Westminster during recent years, and my earnest hope is that it may be rightly understood and valued by the public. But besides this I have an experience, and the facts of that experience will worry the mere deductions made, often from incomplete data, by "the practical man." To begin at the beginning. I was born on the Christmas Day of a very hard winter in the decade immediately following "the Hungry Forties," into a family which ultimately numbered thirteen (unlucky number) and with a bad horoscope. It would seem then that I was foredoomed to a rough time with fate, and I was. My schooldays ended when I was about eight years of age, my attainments at school amounting to little more than the Lord's Prayer, the alphabet, and the multiplication table. With this mental outfit I set out to make a living in a world created by Adam Smith. Of course the Lord's Prayer was not practical in an economic regime, where "the social affections are accidental and disturbing elements." The multiplication table I found uninteresting, just cold, callous facts. The alphabet, however, had possibilities. My mother was imaginative and emotional. She loved music and poetry, and was well versed in the wisdom literature of the Bible. She had ideals. My father was stern, logical, industrious, practical. He had ideas. I was an impressionable youth and sensitive to the difference of these two types of character, both admirable in their places, but I gave the higher place to that of my mother. The point is this, that there are other places than schools where things are learned. The home influence is of vastly more importance for education than mere instruction in elementary schools. It is therefore a wise policy to educate parents that they may educate their children: for there is no teacher like a mother. Love is greater than logic, and it is better to feel than to know.

I was well on in manhood before I took seriously to systematic study. Finding myself woefully behind what I felt I ought to be, I resolved to make an effort to mend my condition. But how? No municipal science and art schools then existed in the town in which I still live; no University Extension nor W.E.A. Tutorial Classes; only Popular Lectures at the Y.M.C.A. I decided to attend these, and they deepened my determination. It was a strange delight to me to hear the lecturer on astronomy tell the wonderful story of the stars. How I envied him as he dexterously chalked his diagrams, and how I yearned to understand the cryptic characters of the press-man who reported him. I bought a shorthand book and taught myself shorthand with such proficiency as to be appointed teacher at the Y.M.C.A. class. This was to me at once a triumph and an encouragement. Spurred on by this success, I bought a celestial globe and learned to work out "Keith's Problems," and I have loved to roam in the sky ever since. Some time ago, a very practical friend of mine was advising me to "drop this nonsense, and begin to do something that would bring some pleasure into my life; to make money." "Look at me," he said, "I have been to Paris for a month." "My dear sir," I answered, "You are a very good fellow, but when you speak of 'nonsense' you speak nonsense, and when you speak of pleasure you have no idea of it. To Paris forsooth! Why, sir, I take week-end trips to the Milky Way, and it would be futile to attempt to describe to you the pleasure I get from these cosmic excursions."

Twenty-five years ago, that enthusiast, Miss Rigby, secretary of the local branch of University Extension, insistently urged me to take a ticket for a course of Extension lectures. I hesitated and invented excuses for refusing. I felt that I should find myself surrounded by consciously superior people, from which class I had already caught many a chill. She persisted, and ultimately succeeded in persuading me. I went to the first lecture and discovered to my great surprise how much I had misjudged, as it has been so frequently misjudged, the spirit and conduct of University Extension. The humanness and sympathy of the lecturer, the goodwill and kindness of the committee, the comradeship and helpfulness of the members, at once won my regard and have sustained it ever since. These are facts and are quite practical to everybody except the practical man. Do not misunderstand me. I do not say that men should not be practical. We must all be practical or perish. I do not gird at those earnest men who ended the superstitions of the alchemists and gave a practical turn to research by applying the inductive method to their investigations, and ushering in the age of discovery and invention which, under an ideal commercial and political system, might have done so much more for the race. No! my contempt is for the suckling of Capitalism who translates life into terms of the Stock Exchange, who would pawn the dirty rags of his soul for a glass of sour wine and a vile cigar, and sneer at the sentimentality of Ruskin because he loved his mother. I was shocked to read in a recent newspaper, that a professor of mathematics had described a learned defence of the Classics in schools as "glorified clap-trap." These are not the men to entrust with the direction of education. They do not understand it. We must get some sentiment into the national life. The great need of the present hour is the poet, not the politician, the prophet, not the priest.

It was my good fortune to begin my University Extension career with a course of lectures on Greek History from Solon to Pericles. What a joy it brought into my life to watch Athens rise to the zenith of Greek civilisation. Hundreds of hours have I gloated over the victories of Marathon and Salamis. And those Olympic festivals—the thrilling excitement of the chariot race, and the pageantry of the pan-athenaic procession in which Miltiades, thrice-victor, was carried to the Acropolis to be crowned with a garland of bay-leaves. Talk about national sentiment! I have been the winner of that chariot race many a time when I have tackled a task apparently beyond me. Then, as if to add joy to joy, that most delightful expounder of Greek life, Mr Kaines Smith, delivered two courses of lectures, one on Greek Religion and Architecture, and one on Greek Art and National Life. Thrills? Who can ever forget the gesture and the eloquence with which he described the Discobolus? Of course one never does forget. And that skilled exponent of physical science, the late Douglas Carnegie, an experimentalist with almost wizard-like dexterity, lectured on "the Forces of Nature," "Light and Sight." That I may give some idea of the scope of

University Extension culture, and the quality of teaching, I beg for toleration in giving this list of names. It is a great delight to me even to write them.

Dr Cranage on Architecture (Gothic); the Rev. T. E. R. Phillips on the Solar System; Dr Wicksteed on Dante; Harold Williams on Shakespeare; Hamilton Thompson on Chaucer; Ian Hannah on India; Mr Wyatt on English Literature; Dr Markham Lee on Music; J. E. Phythean on Pictures; Mr Barkway on 18th century writers; F. Hutchinson on National Life, and a dozen others. And I, a working-man, I am the product of the intellectual workmanship of these good men. But what was involved in the making? They have put me in communion with the greatest minds of the world's great ages; they have made me companion of the poets; they have tuned my ear to the sweetest music, and opened my eyes to beauties indescribable. They have given me the power of transport to the margin of the universe. Facts? You poor little farthing trumpet-blowers who go to Paris for a month, you don't know you are born. I wouldn't change my condition for the wealth of any millionaire. I am having the joy of life that was denied to me in the years of my youth.

But I must say something about University Extension method, which, in my opinion, is especially adapted to working-men students. The subjects are arranged in educational sequence—three years in arts and one in science. The history, politics and arts of a period are taken in immediate succession. There are two terms of 12 lectures in a session. The lectures are of one hour's duration. The students make notes and each may write an essay on a question put by the lecturer. The essays are corrected by the lecturer and marks allowed according to merit. There is a students' class in which discussion is carried on between lecturer and students. At the end of the term there is an examination in which the student may pass or gain honours, in which case he obtains a certificate. After completing eight terms and passing the examinations, he may write an essay, the subject of which is suggested by the Syndicate, and if successful, he obtains the Vice-Chancellor's certificate and gives it to his only son with pride. It will be seen then that the work is thorough. Now that is a diarist kind of statement. Let me get back to the spirit. There is a University Extension atmosphere and the moment one breathes it he becomes human. It is the most democratic organisation in the world. All distinctions of social status, all consciousness of class, vanish immediately one breathes University Extension air. There is the most complete co-operation and comradeship it is possible to get with human material. To crown all, there is that most delightful gathering, the Summer Meeting, where friends of kindred spirit meet in joyous mood to hear lectures by the greatest scholars of the day and to peep in at the banqueting halls of intellectual life and traditional glory, at Oxford and Cambridge.

We have just passed through the greatest struggle of history, and the sum of reaction is not yet computable. Much will have to be done ere the foundations of reconstruction can be bedded for the erection of a noble structure which shall be the glory of England and a pattern for the world.

I said that University Extension is especially adapted to the needs and opportunities of the workers. Let me say something about the Workers' Educational Association. I joined the Association at the beginning of its existence and for eight years I have been a student in a W.E.A. Tutorial Class. The method of the Tutorial Class is similar to that of University Extension—one hour's lecture, one hour's discussion on the subject-matter of the lecture, and the writing of essays for the lecturer. There is this difference, however, that the number of students is limited to thirty-two, and the lecture is a class lecture as distinct from a public lecture. The lecturer can therefore go into greater detail and more closely reasoned explanations than would be possible with a large audience. This, of course, arouses keen discussion such as often taxes the knowledge and ingenuity of the tutor to sum up and pronounce a verdict upon. The subject for study is chosen by the students themselves; but once chosen it is studied for a period of not less than three years. There are twenty-four weekly classes in each of three sessions, and the quality of teaching is of University standard. It will be seen then that the study is intensive. Economics and history appear to be the subjects most generally chosen. Now the W.E.A. was an offshoot of University Extension, and carries on the grand spirit of comradeship and co-operation which characterises the parent movement. The keen desire for knowledge is very marked in the Tutorial Class. There is real earnestness among the students. In the intervals between sessions, in most centres, there are 'rambles" and inter-branch rallies, and these are not merely picnics but serious work.

It is a sight for the gods to see W.E.A. students at play. The springs of mirth flood the swamps of austerity and break down the fences of conventionalism. Laughter-de-luxe is the brand of W.E.A. hilarity. The rambles usually take place on Saturday afternoons. Out to the fields, parks, and villages, a happy band of light-hearted men and women wend their way to look at mother nature in her summer clothes. Sometimes an expert will accompany us with microscope and vasculum and explain the life-history of green hydra, or some of the magnificent mosses. At other times an artist will talk about the orchestration of colour, or an architect interpret the form and decoration of some old village church. A geologist has taken us miles along the shore to explain silting and coast-erosion. We have learned about the carbonisation of coal at the corporation gas-works, and electricity at the municipal generating station. We have studied the periodicity of the rainfall at the meteorological observatory, and observed sun-spots through the great telescope; an annual inter-branch rally at the Liverpool University introduces us to the wonderful devices for the transforming of energy. The joy of these rambles is "better felt than tell't." They are an expression of the spirit which characterises the whole movement throughout the land, and their educational value is beyond rubies.

It is worthy of serious consideration, whether our country does not demand a new order of intellect, and whether the workers cannot furnish a vast amount of materials. It is not greater power to produce that is needed, nor a pious conception of citizenship. It is not growth of intellect, purity of taste, nor even character that is wanted. It is all these united. Every educated man is under great responsibilities to bring into the light and foster all the talent which comes under his influence.

Vast treasures of thought, of noble feeling, of pure aspirations, exist among the workers quite unknown to practical politicians, which have never been called forth because opportunity has been lacking. We never can tell how much has been lost to mankind through social barriers being set up to hinder the free development of man's best nature. To provide intellectual and moral sustenance for the people requires an enlargement of thought and an expansiveness of feeling such as have never yet been shown. The nation needs wisdom and understanding exceeding much, and largeness of heart even as sands on the sea-shore. How pitiable are the quarrels of politicians as to who shall be the leader, and playing the low-down game in order to dish the opposition! Even religious denominations split on the turning of theological pin-points. How futile! How silly! We must take our stand on fundamental principles, and set the wheels in motion, which, in their revolution, will spread life, and light, and joy through the land. Here in this grand old country let the tide of ignorance be stayed; let the flame of human intellect rise, and sweetly mingle with the source of all mental light and beauty, purified by the highest influences of faith and love. We must bring to this great work every capability of mind and heart, and with an ever increasing strength we may build a city fit for heroes to live in.

I have finished my task; I have told my tale. I know that it is not a model of literary craftsmanship, perhaps not even quite logical. Refinement counts for little in an "S.O.S." emergency, and logic is an affair of pedants. It is because I love men and women that I have snatched a few hours at intermittent intervals to plead for my brothers and sisters at this time of national reconstruction.

What the workers need most is knowledge and wisdom, and the time will surely come when they will possess them. Then, and not till then, shall we see the Canaan for which we have hoped so long. When we can stand together and claim our heritage; when we can stand shoulder-to-shoulder, with our eyes open, and our faces to the light; when we can stand in solid phalanx, hand clasped in hand, and declare with one united voice that never again shall ignorance and vice darken our minds and blight our lives, nor our children lack tenderness and love. When we can belt the equator with the bond of human brotherhood, and chant the song of love, then the lads and lasses of the forge and the mill, having laid down their tasks, can jaunt joyfully together, and with light heart and mirthful laughter dance merrily upon the green sward, mayhap beneath which are resting in peace the bones of some pioneer who lived to make that dancing possible. Then

> New arts shall rise of loftier mould,
> And mightier music fill the skies,
> And every life shall be a song,
> And all the earth be paradise.

# INDEX

Devon County Council and U.E., 177
Drama, the, 30 f., 46

East London Naturalist Club, 40
**Economics,** 27, 53, 118, 144; theory and morality, 211
**Education,** Acts 1899, 56; 1902, 56, 66; 1918, 3, 83, 85, 156, 177 f.; aim of, 209, 212; authorities and voluntary effort, 6; books and, 108; character and, 92; elementary and higher, 37 f.; experience and, 48, 132; freedom and, 10; an interpretation of life, 97, 213; lifelong, 3, 17 f.; nature of, 209; meaning of, 16 f.; necessary for public service, 22, 93, 108 f.; policy of, 9; political responsibility and, 93; remedy for class consciousness, 92; right to, 208; special and general, 118 f.; tradition established, 119; voluntary character of, in England, 5, 67; of working people, 111
English tradition in education, 5, 9, 66
Evening classes, 41, 52, 56, 68
Exeter College, 164
Exhibition, the Great 1851, 42

Fellowship, sense of, 6 f., 32, 38, 39, 43 f., 45, 54, 97, 107 f., 220 f.
Finance, 61, 103, 126, 170, 175
Fircroft College, 122
Firth College, Sheffield, 163
**Franchise** and education, 90, 93, 112; women's, 134
**Freedom and Government,** 9 f.; in education, 10, 70 f.
Friendly Societies, 113, 116
**Friends, Society of,** 42, 54; and colleges, 76

Gilchrist Lectures, 47 n., 167, 176
Greenhow College, 152

Harvey, Lord Arthur, 157
Heart and intellect, 210
History, 26 f., 37, 53, 103, 118, 144, 165, 192
Hole, James, 50

Ignorance, dangers of, 208
Individual, value of the, 212
Industrial revolution, the, 42
Industry, reorganisation of, 121
Infant welfare centres, 143
Ipswich College, 45

Joint committees, A.E., 59, 81, 84 f., 89; of L.E.A., 127 f., 188

**Labour,** bias not necessarily involved, 130; its contribution to learning, 48, 132; experience the basis of a new culture, 111, 129 f., 131; movement, 51, 112, 120; organisations educative, 105, 111, 113, 118, 120, 141; Universities and, 56, 101 f., 106 f.; U.E. and, 105; women, 142
Labour College, the, 61, 68, 71, 73, 123, 124 f.
Labour Party, the, 121
Languages, 37
**Lectures,** conditions of value, 50, 83, 103; courses of, 162, 171; decline of interest, 49; short courses, 163
Lecturers, provision for, 178
Leeds, University, 163; workmen, 39
Legislation and conditions of self-improvement, 112
Leicester College, 45
Leicester C.C. and U.E., 177 f.